# MARGE'S MUSINGS

Marjorie Alumbaugh

UTILIS EST AD METAM

PUBLISHING

# Marge's Musings

Marjorie Alumbaugh

# Preface

It was Marge's desire to publish a collection of her poems.

We hope this book provides a glimpse of the person she was

as she shared her thoughts, feelings, and faith,

writing her journey through the seasons of life.

# INTRODUCTION

I'm the Grandma Moses of poetry;
  I share my feelings in rhyme.
I write of the changing of seasons;
  The yearly cycle of time.

I write of my friends and my family;
  Share memories from days that are past.
There are so many things to discourse on;
  The range of subjects is vast.

I base many poems on scripture;
  Often God puts the thoughts in my head.
I write during times of worship;
  Summarizing the words that are said.

I write for special occasions;
  Each Christmas I make my own card.
With so many aspects of Jesus,
  It's a task that is not at all hard.

I write for funerals and weddings;
  Any family special event.
I write of vacations and travel
  And sleeping outdoors in a tent.

Life is such a vast landscape;
   There are many word pictures to paint.
I want to share some of my vision;
   But I know a true artist I ain't.

If I have any talents,
   God has bestowed them on me.
I strive to follow His leading
   To be what He'd have me to be.

As I share insights God gives me;
   One thing is certainly true.
God's word is as old as creation
   But each day I find... something new.

                              --MEA

# CONTENTS

# Nature

# *Time*

# America

# Love

God Is Love!

True Love

In Marriage

The Dumpster

Pleasures, Possessions, Position

Hurt in the Family

Second Opportunities

Tough Love

Being a Grandmother

God's Love

# *Family*

# Memories

# *Life*

# Faith

# Nature

# GOD'S CREATION

In springtime, the season of planting,

  Or in autumn, when gathering the grain,

In days of sunshine and breezes,

  Or the times when it's stormy with rain.


In winter, fields barren and dormant

  Awaiting new growth to appear,

Whatever the time or the season

  God has control through the year.


Much of life is a mystery;

  God created all things that grow.

Though man's knowledge increases;

  There is much he will never know.


God made all of creation

  And then its goodness declared.

All things were made to His measure;

  This earth for mankind prepared.

# SOWING TO REAP

*Galatians 6: 7-10*

Some things cannot be changed;

   This is a season for sowing.

We later will reap the harvest;

   The seeds which we plant begin growing.


There are some things that can be changed;

   The field where we are planting.

By sowing in the spirit's realm,

   The harvest God will be granting.


We can choose how much to sow;

   To lavishly plant with our hand

That we may gain a rich harvest

   Reaping when God shall command.


We can choose to continue our sowing

   From youth to elderly days.

The seeds which we plant can flourish

   And spread in so many ways.

# MY GARDEN

A work in progress; always something to do
   But my spirits are lifted as my garden I view.
From Spring's earliest crocus to the asters of fall
   From the ground cover ivy to the sunflowers so tall.

A scene always changing; surprises each day
   While another plant grows, early blooms fade away.
Black-eyed susans and cone-flowers
which some would call weeds
   Mixed with zinnias and marigolds I've grown from seeds.

Hostas and ferns flourish under the trees
   While the lilies and phlox attract lots of bees.
Swings for the grandkids "flying up to the sky;"
   A creek where small fish are seen flitting by.

Bird houses available for building a nest;
   But a home on the porch wren families like best.
From a modified pump a fountain can flow;
   Steadily streaming to a large tub below.

Back in a corner is the vegetable plot
   That starts to produce when the weather gets hot.
Potatoes, tomatoes and tall stalks of corn,
   Zucchini vines bearing new squash every morn.

A garden is soothing and peaceful to me
   For in it God's presence I feel.
He's the Master; I'm just the apprentice
   And for me it's a wonderful deal.

# THE SPIDER WEBS

One morning it was foggy;
   There was moisture in the air.
Spider webs so intricate
   Were sparkling everywhere.

They dangled from the power lines;
   And the clothes line had its share.
How hard the spiders must have worked;
   Such beauty to prepare!

They were anchored to the fence posts
   And adorned an old lawn chair;
Each tree limb had its ornament
   Like jewels prized and rare.

Each pattern was so perfect;
   Each strand was in its place.
Each individual masterpiece
   Resembled Belgian lace.

Then soon the sun came breaking out
   To drive the fog away;
But still I call up visions
   Of that rare and gorgeous day.

# THE RAINBOW

God made a covenant with all living things;
  With mankind, with beast and with birds.
"No more will floods ravage the earth"
  To Noah these were His words.

A rainbow's appearance in the clouds of the sky
  Is a sign, God's reminder to man
Of the covenant He created
  Revealing His love through His plan.

To us, a beautiful rainbow
  Is a visible message from God;
To encourage and uplift our spirits
  As through daily routine we plod.

Winter is long, cold and dreary;
  Nights are lengthy and daytime is brief.
The bright skies and warmth of the springtime
  Are such a joyous relief.

Flowers in brilliant profusion;
  Blooming shrubs like gigantic bouquets;
Scenes reflecting God's glory
  Whatever direction we gaze.

Dark clouds on the horizon;
  Sudden showers that cleanse and renew.
Then the arc of a breathtaking rainbow
  As streams of sunshine break through.

All of life has its seasons
  We treasure events that are rare.
A rainbow after a deluge
  Reminds us that God is still there.

In the midst of complete dissolution
   When all of the landscape is trashed.
In the loss of lives and possessions
   Our hopes and ambitions are smashed.

We question why God has allowed it.
   Is it possible He's unaware
Of the havoc that ravished His people?
   To allow it, does He not care?

Such doubtings are our human nature
   And we ask God to give us a sign.
We need reassurance and comfort
   From a God who is Holy, divine.

While we wait, we can seek our own rainbow;
   A small one that floats in the air
Because of the sunlight's reflection;
   A promise that God is still there.

In science we learn about prisms,
   Of wave lengths, refraction of light
But when we see a beautiful rainbow
   We humbly thank God for the sight.

A rainbow, a hope and a promise
   From God, His original art.
Just a fragment of His creation
   That awes and touches our heart.

We sometimes must seek our own rainbow
   Or remember a scene we have viewed.
A rainbow is God's promise to us.
   When we see it, our spirit's renewed.

# MY LIFE-STYLE

My life-style is labor intensive;
  I live in an old-fashioned way.
I grow lots of food in the garden
  Then can it and store it away.

I gather in berries for jellies;
  I do all my baking from scratch.
If someone is hungry for cookies,
  I'm happy to stir up a batch.

My herbs add fragrance and flavor
  To the home-made dishes I serve.
I feel like a pioneer woman;
  Nature's bounty I'm pleased to preserve.

I walk behind a push mower
  Cutting grass on an acre of lawn.
I compost grass clippings and garbage
  So the cycle of growth will go on.

I find it is pure recreation
  To toil on my parcel of ground;
Then see the results of my labors
  When the harvest is spread all around.

I'm pleased to be in tune with nature;
  To sense that God is so near
As I relish the gifts of each season
  And savor each day of the year.

# ATTUNED TO NATURE

Going out primitive camping
  Is an outing to love or detest.
When the gear is all stowed
and the fire has burned low,
  That's the time when I like it best.

Our bodies cast long black shadows
  In reflections from our lantern light;
As its flame is slowly extinguished,
  We become one with the night.

The dew has been silently falling;
  In the hollows and low spots there's mist.
Each blade of grass near our campsite
  By droplets of moisture is kissed.

Through the evening, the moon has been rising
  And now it has topped nearby trees;
Clear blue sky all around it
  As westward it moves by degrees.

Surrounded by sounds of the nighttime
  More audible when we are still
We can hear the crickets, the tree frogs
  And a bird who calls out "whip-poor-will."

As I settle into my bedroll,
  "Who-who" I hear an owl call.
I drift off to sleep with the knowledge
  That God is in charge of it all.

Such camping gives time for reflection;
  Distractions and problems are few;
God's handiwork all about me
  Assuring that His word is true.

And when the camping trip's over,
  I surely will be more aware
That a bathtub is mighty convenient;
  Every home needs a "Lazy-Boy" chair.

# THE WEATHER

If we never like cold weather
  And we grumble about the rain,
Cause the weekends should be sunny
  Does the Lord hear us complain?

He's the Ruler of all nature,
  And it's under His domain.
We should always praise and love Him
  In the sunshine or the rain.

Though the weather may not please us,
  He still will meet our needs;
If we always place our trust in Him,
  And follow where He leads.

# THE JOYS OF JOGGING

Each morning when I get up
  I put on my jogging shoes.
If I don't run at least six miles,
  I haven't "paid my dues."

I see the changing seasons;
  Watch the seedlings sprout and grow;
See them ripen for the harvest;
  Followed by the ice and snow.

I see the squirrels and rabbits
  Frolic as they run and play.
Sometimes I glimpse a whitetail deer
  Which swiftly leaps away.

I see the ducks and geese in flight
  Stretched out across the sky;
And after they are lost from view
  Still hear the haunting cry.

I look at God's creation
  And I breathe a word of prayer.
I sense that God cares for me;
  Is with me everywhere.

He gives me strength to run each mile;
  He gives me eyes to see.
The thought is overwhelming
  That He's always there for me.

While running I can worship,
  God hears thought as well as speech.
When I meditate on nature,
  God uses it to teach.

Sometimes I get an insight
  Into things that worry me.
God gives me reassurance
  And my spirits are set free.

# FOG

Layers of fog can cover the earth;
  So filmy and yet quite opaque.
To disregard its potential
  Would certainly be a mistake.

So sheer and yet with such substance;
  It becomes an impenetrable veil.
It drifts with such ease o'er the landscape
  With long, snaky tendrils which trail.

Pale and pristine in its beauty,
  So languidly drifting about;
Seeking each creek and each valley,
  Filling and blotting them out.

It alters our visual perception;
  Our world seems shallow and flat.
It limits our power of discernment,
  Blurring the scene where we're at.

Fog -- the silent encroacher;
  It blankets the world from our view.
Each time I see it I marvel
  At the wonderful things God can do.

# HARVEST TIME

Each year there's a harvest,
  A season to gather,
Abundant or sparse
  Due to seasonal weather.

Planting in springtime
  We watch the crop grow.
We hope for an increase
  In all that we sow.

Floods, drought and heat waves
  May hamper production.
When the harvest is gathered,
  There is a reduction.

If the harvest is ample
  And the season's just right
The bounty is gathered
  By day and by night.

When the harvest is over,
  We each have a reason
To give thanks to God
  For the gifts of the season.

The harvest -- a blessing,
  Fruits, vegetables, grain.
As the excess is stored,
  God's goodness is plain.

# LATE AUTUMN

We took our dog out walking
  Just before we went to bed.
We enjoyed the pleasant landscape;
  "Autumn's beautiful," we said.

The night was warm but breezy;
  Clouds were scudding 'cross the moon.
We basked in all the beauty
  Which we knew would vanish soon.

We woke in early morning
  To the pitter-pat of rain.
The sound of distant thunder
  Lulled us back to sleep again.

The day was slow in breaking
  And the landscape was more gray.
The ground with leaves was littered;
  Autumn's glory cast away.

The trees appeared as skeletons;
  Each limb outlined and clear.
Their leafy plumage stripped away
  To wait the coming year.

The bitter winds will follow
  With the threat of killing frost.
One night of freezing temperatures;
  And plant growth will be lost.

Autumn's warmth and vivid colors
  Will vanish for this year;
But the splendor of this season
  In my memory will be clear.

# A THANKSGIVING PRAYER

At dusk, I ventured from my house
  And breathed the crisp, fresh air.
I viewed the muted landscape;
  And voiced a silent prayer.

For dried and withered fallen leaves
  That crunched beneath my feet.
While others strewn like golden coins
  Were scattered in the street.

For cornstalks crushed and flattened
  Since the harvest's gathered in.
For fields brown and fallow
  Till the springtime comes again.

For cattails growing in the mud;
  A place for geese to rest;
To shelter till tomorrow
  On their migratory quest.

For setting sun in western sky
  And lingering glow of light.
As darkness filters o'er the scene,
  Day is replaced by night.

For vision to survey the scene;
  God's autumn patchwork quilt.
For feelings to appreciate
  What nature is about.

For chilly winds of evening
  Which drive me back inside
To warm and cozy shelter
  Where I'm happy to reside.

For blessings in profusion;
  More than I can ever count.
Such overflowing bounty
  Is what God's love is about.

# A TASTE OF WINTER

The day was cold and windy;

  There were waves upon the lake.

I met the wind's resistance

  With every step I'd take.


The animals had vanished

  To a warmer nest or den.

I saw no other joggers;

  Just two telephone maintenance men.


The geese had found a sheltered cove;

  Put heads beneath a wing.

As they ruffled up their feathers,

  Did they long for days of spring?


Winds howling through the treetops

  Seemed to shout with mighty voice,

"This is the day that God has made.

  Accept it and rejoice!"

# WINTERTIME ARTISTRY

There is magic in God's creation;
  His artistry truly unique.
His landscapes are ever changing
  With beauty each day of the week.

As the curtains of darkness are parted
  Revealing the onset of day,
Sometimes wisps of fog tend to linger
  Till the sunbeams drive them away.

With frost God can paint such a vista;
  Add dimension to each bush or tree;
Turn lawns into crisp, white shag carpets;
  Icy patterns on windows we see.

Flakes of snow are the jewels of winter
  As softly they flutter around.
Such gems of delicate beauty
  Can collect till they cover the ground.

But sometimes the clouds are so heavy
  The day is a monotone, gray.
The landscape is softened and muted;
  The color has all drained away.

God's handiwork is ever changing;
  Each day is a gift He bestows.
As we savor the beauty around us,
  Our spirit of thankfulness grows.

# MEDITATIONS IN NATURE

A skim of ice upon the lake;
  With snow like frosting on a cake.

The sun arising from its bed;
  A fiery ball of orange and red.

The clouds all tinged in pink and gold;
  I watched the morning scene unfold.

A heron awkward while at rest;
  In flight was filled with gracefulness.

My breath expelled in puffs of steam;
  I seemed to travel through a dream.

A moment I shall not reclaim;
  A picture only God could frame.

A special time God shared with me;
  This view of peace and harmony.

# REFLECTIONS ON A SNOWFALL

Picture postcard perfect
  Was the wintry scene today.
Adhering to each surface,
  A coat of fresh snow lay.

Footsteps crunching in the snowfall,
  Made a squeaky, rhythmic sound.
The snow, a velvety curtain
  Still falling all around.

Muted gray tones of the landscape
  Were a contrast to the snow.
The sky, a bowl of gray above,
  Lake water gray below.

The lake mirrored reflections
  Of the trees along its shore.
The snow became a carpet
  For the coastline's rugged floor.

The road a long, black ribbon
  Cut across the peaceful view.
An outlet to the busy world
  With all its things to do.

The beauty of the landscape
  Softened by the falling flakes,
Reminded me how God forgives
  And covers our mistakes.

As pure and white as any snow,
  God's love for all mankind.
By observing scenes of nature
  Truths eternal I can find.

# THE PROMISE OF DAWN

A dome of gray with streaks of white

    Proclaims the coming close of night.

In eastern sky the slightest fringe

    Of color with a rosy tinge.


In western sky the moon is pale

    Covered by the sheerest veil.

Retreating from the coming day,

    Silently it slips away.


The trees are outlined, tall and dark

    Against the skyline, looming stark.

The rising sun is hid from view;

    Till ragged clouds let it shine through.


Last days of winter still may cling;

    But in the dawn I sense the spring.

Reminded that since time began,

    Changing seasons were God's plan.

# THE EASTER LILY

The days are becoming much shorter;
  The growing season has passed.
The warmth of the sun does not linger;
  The chill of twilight comes fast.

The frost has killed vegetation.
  Plants are wilted; can't hold up a head.
Although I know life is dormant,
  It's depressing to see things look dead.

We are digging the leeks and the turnips;
  Capping roses so they won't freeze;
Mulching leaves which fall in profusion
  Making skeletons out of the trees.

Gathering seeds from the zinnias
  To plant them again in the spring.
I'm looking beyond the dark winter
  To what a new season will bring.

I take a last stroll through the garden;
  Discover a marvelous thing.
An Easter lily is blooming
  Its blossoms so white and pristine.

I had set it out only last April;
  Discarded when Easter was through.
It had withered and soon been forgotten
  And now it is blooming anew.

Symbolic of our resurrection
  A lily is blooming in fall
Reminding that God rules all nature
  And He's in control of us all.

# SEASONS OF LIFE

In each year there are four seasons;
  Each person's life has seasons too.
Each season is different, brings changes
  With challenging things we can do.

In winter the landscape is dormant.
  Each day is bone-chilling and bleak.
By drawing nearer to Jesus,
  We find the warmth that we seek.

Spring brings new life, a renewal;
  Causing plants that are dormant to grow.
God's word in our hearts start to flourish
  Mush as unseen roots neath the snow.

Summer is a time for maturing;
  All living things have a growth span.
Christians who study the scriptures
  Also mature, it's God's plan.

In autumn we bring in the harvest;
  Culmination of seasons of toil.
The plants have flourished and ripened
  Because they fell in good soil.

Jesus often gave illustrations
  Citing nature and seasonal things;
The diligence of a good farmer
  And the bountiful harvest it brings.

Each human life has its season
  From newborn, perhaps through old age.
But life is always uncertain,
  May end whatever its stage.

We each can enjoy our season;
  Make the best of our quota of days
By living our lives to the fullest;
  Praising God for His marvelous ways.

This earth has had many seasons;
  Twelve months comprising each year;
But the time of Jesus' returning
  Each season, is growing more near.

Time

# A NEW YEAR

Another year is ended;
  Was it wasted or well spent?
Time is irretrievable;
  We wonder where it went.

We can't retrieve the days or hours;
  The past we cannot alter.
By dwelling on our past defeats;
  We hesitate and falter.

The new year with allotted time
  We can so wisely spend.
By setting goals to grow with God;
  His kingdom to defend.

By seeking Christian attributes
  To nourish and sustain,
We're fortified for daily life
  In happiness or pain.

Time well spent in Godly tasks
  Is like a priceless treasure.
Time expended in such work
  Is blessed in endless measure.

# A MINUTE

Did you ever stop to wonder
  Just at one certain minute
Of all the things that minute holds
  And your position in it?

Each minute is original;
  No two are quite the same;
And one particular minute
  We cannot hold or claim.

A minute seems so very small;
  A tiny building block.
Sixty needed to become an hour;
  They're the basics of each clock.

A minute is just long enough
  For good news or a surprise;
And a minute holds much beauty
  If we open up our eyes.

Because a scene's familiar,
  We may overlook a sight
At the dawning of the morning
  Or the lingering dusk of night.

Just a minute for awareness
  Of the wonders of creation.
A minute of reflection
  Can make a great impression.

A minute doing routine tasks
  That chance to come our way;
Dispensing smiles and friendly words
  To those we meet each day.

A minute for preparing
  To have a change of heart;
To gives our lives to Jesus;
  To make a brand new start.

A minute to depart this life;
  For earthly time to end;
Or else we'll see the minute
  When Christ Jesus will descend.

A minute is important
  And we need to be aware
Through the joy or pain each minute holds
  We can know that God is there.

# STAGES IN THE LIFE OF A WOMEN

There are stages of life, Shakespeare has said
  And I'm sure that's undoubtedly true.
Relationships change as we go through each one.
  Let's go back, recalling a few.

Our first interaction's with Mother
  Or a caregiver helping a while.
If we're warm, fed, dry and cuddled,
  We are quick to respond with a smile.

We have play dates with friends or cousins;
  Are taught to take turns and play fair.
In grade school boys are a nuisance;
  With girlfriends (BFF), our secrets we share.

Then KABOOM we're hit by lightning!
  The love of our life we have found.
If he smiles when we meet in the hallway,
  We are walking on air, not the ground.

Writing his name in our notebooks;
  Making plans of which he's unaware.
The ups and downs of such romance
  Is almost too much to bear!

The next step is actual dating;
  At ball games, a movie, or dance.
In High School some make connections
  That lead to a life-long romance.

Next is engagement, then marriage.
  Commitment, a pledge and a vow.
Looking forward to days filled with pleasure,
  Overcoming all problems somehow.

Then a couple are joined by a baby.
  It is loved, but the difference it brings --
A family of three needs a schedule
  For a child requires many things.

With each year, life is more hectic;
  Other children may come on the scene.
Schooling, athletics and music
  For an adolescent or teen.

Then, suddenly kids have all grown;
  Moved out to a place of their own.
For Mom and Dad it's all over;
  Empty house and they're all alone.

Good years for hobbies and traveling,
  Exercising or taking a class.
Eager for perks of retirement;
  How quickly these years seem to pass.

Most folks celebrate anniversaries;
  Fifty years is often the goal.
Health problems are part of the picture;
  A lifetime has taken its toll.

Time keeps moving forward
  As hearing and eyesight grow dim.
All of life is a learning experience;
  More days have been happy than grim.

When we are disabled and helpless,
  We know for the whole course we've stayed.
We are thankful to just be together
  For each other's comfort and aid.

# THE TIME OF A MAN

A man is as small as a grain of sand
  Or a drop of rain in the sea.
A moment of time on the stage of life
  In the winds waits eternity.

His time is as short as a nod of the head,
  Or a smile, or a blink of an eye.
He'll never accomplish all he might want
  No matter how much he shall try.

The tides of history will roll over man.
  A moment and then he is gone.
Perhaps he is missed for a very short time
  But still the world marches on.

How fleeting the moment of earthly life.
  Eternity waits in the wings.
Possessions do not go with him;
  How worthless are "valuable" things!

To know the things with true value
  Is the sign of a man who is wise.
Laying up treasures in Heaven
  Assures him of winning the prize.

A wise man uses his moment;
  Reaches out and takes the Lord's hand.
He walks steadfastly through hardships
  And follows his Savior's command.

He knows that things work together
  For good for the called of the Lord.
He steps out on faith when he falters
  And bravely wields his God's sword.

As the curtain of life is descending,
  He's at peace as it comes to an end.
For a much better life is beginning
  With Jesus, his Savior and friend.

# MARRIAGE

Have you noted how at weddings
  older ladies shed some tears?
They are happy for the couple
  but they also have some fears.

No one can see the future;
  they don't know what lies ahead.
Fairy tales have happy endings;
  life has ups and downs instead.

Life requires much perseverance
  so a pair can stay the course;
Working through each situation,
  sometimes better, sometimes worse.

Always striving for improvement
  as two share an earthly bond;
Wanting good things for each other
  in the lifetime and beyond.

There are routine tasks and work to do;
  an alarm clock starts the day;
But just waking up together
  makes everything okay.

Creating a foundation
  for family yet to be;
Merging customs and traditions
  is a fundamental key.

A child is a blessing
  to increase a couple's joy.
What can be more precious
  than a baby girl or boy?

Children are a blend of families;
  in appearance, talents, skills.
Looking at their sleeping children;
  hearts with gratitude God fills.

The years go by so quickly;
  children grow, are on their own.
Then again it's just one couple;
  residing all alone.

The months and years keep passing,
  with changes all the way;
Still the vows of the wedding
  are to honor and obey.

As more of life is in the past,
  there are memories to recall.
He sees a slim blonde beauty;
  she sees him standing tall.

When attending other weddings,
  it reminds them of their day;
Now she's the older lady,
  brushing drops of tears away.

# PERSPECTIVE

When I was young, misunderstood
  Adults were out of touch;
But now that I have aged myself
  Old folks have learned so much.

Now youth think I'm the misinformed;
  Wrapped in a mental haze.
Whatever lessons I have learned
  Were in some long gone days.

Our realities are different;
  My views are from the past.
The question that I ask myself,
  "How did life go by so fast?"

I know my grandkids love me
  But I'm such a dinosaur.
They think that I'm stuck in the past;
  No longer know the score.

They see my life as dull and drab;
  The same routine each day.
I chose to put my family first,
  And my own dreams slipped away.

My core values have not changed
  And I still feel young inside
But I am sixty-years away
  From a nineteen-year-old bride.

# BALLERINA AT BEDTIME

A ballerina at bedtime,
  When visions would dance through my head;
Instead of flannel pajamas,
  I was wearing a tutu instead.

Lithe and light as a fairy;
  I could see the scene in my mind.
Dreams of preadolescence,
  Those were the very best kind.

# THE SEASONS OF A MOTHER

Albums filled with snapshots;
  Some have faded through the years;
But they record a lifetime
  Bringing smiles, nostalgic tears.

Albums filled with memories
  Record the generations;
Nephews, nieces, sons and daughters
  All are part of our relations.

Grandma, grandpa, sisters, brothers
  All are on the family tree;
But the father and the mother
  Lead and guide each family.

Motherhood has many stages
  So let's picture just a few.
Starting with expectant mother
  When first baby soon is due.

Baby days at first seem endless;
  But the nights are longer yet.
Just when Mom thinks baby's sleeping
  Then she hears it start to fret.

But looking back in retrospect
  The baby days went fast;
And everybody is relieved
  When potty training's past.

About the age of five or six
  The kids have full-day schooling
With scouts and sports and music too,
  Mom always is car-pooling.

Preteens seek independence;
  Need acceptance by their crowd.
Wearing clothing like all the others,
  Playing music much too loud.

Then too soon a daughter's dating;
  Off she's going to the prom.
Says while walking out the doorway,
  "Needn't wait up for me, Mom."

After high school graduation,
  Children strike out on their own.
College, Army, even marriage,
  Mom is happy that they're grown.

Yet there is a touch of sadness;
  Mother's daily tasks are through.
Till she welcomes her first grandchild;
  And the cycle starts anew.

As she sees grandchildren growing
  And enjoys their progress too,
They know that Grandma loves them
  And is proud of what they do.

Women often become widowed;
  Are alone their final days.
But surrounded by their family;
  They are honored, cherished, praised.

Though the tasks sometimes seem thankless,
  Still a Godly Mother's blessed
Jobs, careers may be important
  But a Mother's role is best.

# OLD AGE

Options narrow as we age;
  Each year we turn another page
Of life, which we cannot reclaim.
  The aging process is its name.

Too old to start a new career,
  So why not be a volunteer?
Tasks of service we can do
  But old folks need a pay check too.

No sympathy from those of youth;
  They are too young to see the truth
That life will quickly pass them by.
  They may not conquer all they try.

Aches and pains come with the years;
  Strength, power and zest then disappears.
Regrets for things too late to alter
  May cause despair so we will falter.

Afraid of chances we could take;
  Afraid of making a mistake
With loss of savings we have gained,
  In cautious living we've been trained.

Victims of our situation;
  We now are old for the duration.
A cause for living we still need
  And future plans which might succeed.

Old age -- some say it is a curse
  But things could often be much worse.
Through memories we can still review;
  Enjoy the things we used to do.

Dream of the way life used to be
  And let our thoughts roam wild and free.
Recall the feeling of our youth
  And for a while deny the truth.

Life always is a finite thing;
  Just as the autumn follows spring.
We are born, we grow, we age, we die;
  To each of us it will apply.

With acceptance comes submission;
  Old age is only a condition.
With loving heart, and inquiring mind;
  Joy in living we can find.

# AGE VERSUS YOUTH

There's a gap between generations;
  Young and old just don't think the same.
Whatever the current dilemma,
  They give each other the blame.

Old folks are rigid and stubborn;
  Out of touch and they haven't a clue.
They are fearful, dispensing dire warnings;
  Always telling the young what to do.

They look to the past as their guidepost;
  Unaware of what lies ahead.
Technology is not their bulwark;
  They cling to their memories instead.

Youth thinks it's time for adventure;
  Life is excitement and fun.
There will be time for commitment
  After their teen years are done.

Everything new is the key word;
  From movies, to music, to style.
Body art such as tattoos and piercings
  May be a big fad for a while.

So much of life is a cycle;
  Each generation the same;
Seeking what's different or shocking;
  Just giving old items new names.

A hoodie is just a sweatshirt
  And a flip-flop was once a thong.

By being a part of the "in" group,
  It feels so good to belong.

The older folks need to remember
  The growing pains of their youth;
Giving the young folks some leeway;
  Distributing kindness, with truth.

Teen years so swiftly are passing;
  Kids need to study, prepare
For the time that is swiftly approaching
  When mother and dad won't be there.

Everyone wants a bright future
  In a land that is noble and fair;
Freedom from crime and oppression;
  Equal rights for all groups everywhere.

We also need to remember
  Life is geared to a fast-moving track.
From youth, to adults, to old folks,
  We proceed - there's no turning back.

We often ponder the question,
  "Where has all of life gone?"
Whatever our age at this moment,
  Let's interact and move on.

If we're young, old age awaits us.
  For the old, young once were we.
We share so much in common;
  Let's be "us" not "you" and "me."

# THE DILEMMA OF BEING 75

Wisdom comes with age
  But youth pay us no heed.
Movement is restricted;
  We no longer move with speed.

There's a change in our appearance;
  Too much weight and wrinkled skin.
If we try to make improvements,
  Where do we begin?

Memory sometimes fails us;
  There are names we can't recall.
But factor in the blessings;
  Life is still good after all.

Our working days are over
  And we get a monthly check.
We still maintain our households;
  Plant some flowers, paint the deck.

Our routine is familiar;
  It's a comfort, not a bore.
We have mates and nearby children.
  Could we really ask for more?

We have a host of memories
  And most of them are good.
Would we choose to change our history
  Even if we could?

# CHANGES

Long stretches of time with what seems no change;

But when we look back, we ponder "how strange."

Change all around us but we could not see;

No awareness, what was, what is, or will be.


Everything grows, people, animals, plants;

From the largest of elephants, to the tiniest of ants.

An invisible process, we change as we grow.

How does it happen? We just do not know.


We see the results, we know change takes place.

A mysterious process, right in front of our face.

For all of men's progress with genes, DNA;

Still so much just happens, God planned it that way.

# HEALTHY AGING

The aging process is part of life
  From the moment when we are born.
Too often we think of the elderly
  As lonely, forsaken, forlorn.

As I age I have gained greater freedom;
  And I've come to really like ME!
I no longer struggle to try to impress
  And the humor in "foul-ups" I see.

I make more time for my interests;
  Am renewed by a walk by the lake.
I savor life's gains and achievements;
  Am less crushed when I make a mistake.

Interaction with others is vital;
  Complimentary words are for free.
To encourage others gives pleasure;
  The recipient's joy pleases me.

I've lowered my expectations;
  No power, no fame, or great wealth.
But I know what is most important,
  My values, my family, my health.

We all know the future's uncertain
  So I strive that each day is well spent.
My motto for life's from the Bible
  "Whatever may be, I'm content."

*(Philippians 4:11)*

# COMMUNICATION

Communication is an art;
  A way for men to share
Some of the details of their life,
  The how, the when, the where.

Cavemen were budding authors
  With stories they could share.
By carving pictures in the rock,
  Left word they had been there.

Indians used puffs of smoke;
  A message in the sky
Another group could fan their fire
  And send a quick reply.

Shipwrecked upon an island;
  Hoping to be found, set free;
The lost sealed notes in bottles
  And tossed them in the sea.

In the days of frontier living
  Travelers took mail to and fro.
From East-coast to California
  Getting news from home was slow.

Progress sometimes seemed sudden;
  Continental railroad track
Made scheduled mailing possible
  From East to West, then back.

When soldiers from this country
  Went to war in foreign lands,
The mail was slow to reach them
  Mired in jungles, swamps or sands.

Messages by telegram
  Brought news of great import.
Families dispersed across the land
  Could get a quick report.

To hear the voice of loved ones
  On a telephone was fine;
But nothing could be private
  With ten families on a line.

Radios for news and drama,
  Weather forecasts, baseball games.
Politicians, entertainers,
  Nationwide were known by name.

Television was a mystery;
  How could far-off scenes appear?
By turning the antenna,
  Pictures sometimes were more clear.

Then satellites went into space
  Beamed images to earth.
Mass communication --
  Just how much is it worth?

Technology seems endless
  With computers and smart phones.
Nothing stays original;
  There are rip-offs, copies, clones.

In just my span of living
  There's been progress, so much change.
Things become familiar
  That once when new, seemed strange.

I've always corresponded
  With my friends, and family too;
Wrote checks, mailed payments for my bills;
  It was the thing to do.

Now a check is so old-fashioned;
  Online banking's how to go.
How secure is information?
  There's no way to really know.

Dependent on social phenomena;
  Each has a personal phone.
A family together for dinner;
  In reality, each is alone.

Lost in their own special interests;
  Conversation, a thing of the past.
Working puzzles, viewing posts or just texting,
  How long will this phase of life last?

Together, but in isolation;
  No time for a personal touch;
Addicted to internet actions
  Informed but still missing so much.

Each child has his own computer;
  No dry facts or learning by rote.
School news is relayed by texting;
  No contact by passing a note.

Drones are the wave of the future;
  Already they track movie stars.
As all of our life is recorded,
  We're imprisoned, though not behind bars.

Communication has always been needed;
  God intended for people to share.
Spontaneously acting with kindness
  Showing others, that for them we care.

There's not time for personal contact;
  A letter, a visit, a call.
One message posted on Facebook
  Will surely take care of it all.

For me, so much change is amazing
  But I know that I'm not alone.
If you want to share what you're feeling,
  Just call me, we'll chat on the phone.

# ONE WEEK

We know that life is uncertain
  And we know that God's in command.
Yet in the routine of our daily life;
  We fully do not understand.

We make our plans for the future;
  This week, this month or next year.
Yet, if the Lord God so chooses
  That future can all disappear.

That Sunday was like many others
  Except for the picnic at four.
I shared with my friends and ate ice cream;
  No thought what the week had in store.

On Monday I took Mom for breakfast;
  We enjoyed the beautiful day.
In the afternoon had a check-up;
  And my cancer exam was okay.

I was thankful for six years remission
  Relieved the procedure was through.
But my body was feeling quire heavy;
  I was dizzy and unbalanced too.

My kids were coming for supper
  With the grandkids staying all night.
But when the family assembled;
  They sensed things with me, were not right.

A blood pressure check was revealing;
  Two hundred over one hundred ten.
Ignoring my protests, denials;
  My family took quick action then.

In emergency I was admitted,
  For treatment and additional testing.
Supported by prayers of family and friends;
  In God's hands my future was resting.

A stroke was the quick diagnosis;
  More tests to pinpoint the cause.
Ultrasounds, MRI and brain scanning
  No definite proof what it was.

A blockage was probably the culprit.
  My symptoms all seemed to fit.
They sent me home with a warning;
  I'd be dizzy and tired for a bit.

In time I should see some improvement;
  The dizziness, weakness should fade.
But if my life needs readjustment
  I'll face it and not be afraid.

Such a week of turmoil, upheaval;
  Form tension to profound relief.
I know God always is with me
  For that is my heartfelt belief.

God will not overload me
  With burdens too much to bear.
I always will cling to that promise
  In times of distress or despair.

The apostle Paul is my mentor.
  He was faithful where'er he was sent.
He will always be my role model;
  Whatever my state, I'm content.

# FULL CIRCLE

When I was just a little girl
  My hair was short and straight.
My mother combed it sleek and smooth
  And said it looked just great.

My sister got the compliments;
  Her hair was red and curly.
I was so shy and silent,
  To strangers I seemed surly.

When I was growing older,
  I tried to change my style.
I slept in rollers every night;
  My routine quite a while.

I thought a perm might help me
  But my hair just turned to frizz.
My mom said leave it natural;
  It's pretty as it is.

I looked through women's magazines
  For beauty hints, suggestion.
My fingers were all thumbs
  As I followed their directions.

A pageboy or a perky flip;
  On models they looked fine.
A headband or a pony-tail
  Were favorite styles of mine.

 In mid-life I admitted
  A stylist I should seek
To tease, arrange my tresses,
  Then spray to hold all week.

That was more convenient
  Till cancer laid me low.
With massive chemo treatments,
  My hair began to go.

Soon it was falling out in clumps;
  My scalp was shining through;
But when the treatments ended,
  In time my new hair grew.

So now I've gone full circle.
  My hair is short and straight,
But now I see things differently
  And think it looks just great!

# PRAISE GOD:
# A BRIGHTER DAY!

I was diagnosed with cancer
  Caught in an early stage.
I went through radiation;
  Marked the days off page by page.

I also took some chemo;
  Five days treatment at a time.
With a battery pack for the energy source
  Pushing medicine through a thin line.

These treatments caused a reaction;
  Sleeplessness, blisters and pain;
But I sensed that God was with me;
  All this agony, yet for gain.

I made a gradual recovery;
  Regained my strength and my hair.
It changed my life for the better;
  Reassured me of God's loving care.

There is no way of knowing the future;
  How long on this earth I'll remain.
But knowing Christ is beside me
  I have faith He will cheer and sustain.

# A QUESTION

The time we live is limited;

Our days on earth are numbered.

How many fresh dawns have I missed

While in my bed I slumbered?

# AUTUMN MUSINGS

The time of harvest is over
  And corn stalks litter the fields.
According to what's been reported,
  The farmers were blessed with high yields.

The evening breezes are chilly
  As darkness creeps over the land.
A reminder that summer is over;
  A seasonal change is at hand.

A time for the fields to lay fallow;
  For birds to depart on their route.
No maps to plan out their journey;
  Their instincts will guide them, no doubt.

Some animals soon will be sleeping
  In a burrow, a pit or a hole.
Some of the creatures that slumber
  Are the chipmunk, the groundhog, the mole.

Many people do not like winter;
  With the ice, the snow and the cold.
We are wise to take safety precautions,
  Especially as we grow old.

God created all of the seasons
  With a purpose, to fulfill his plan.
Seasons to plant, grow and harvest;
  Then rest time for fields and for man.

A time for thanking our maker
  For the blessing of food He provides.
For comforts of light, warmth and bathrooms
  In the homes where each one resides.

A time for being with family;
  Immediate, and distant kin.
With time for reading and sharing,
  It's so good to be bonding again.

A time when we are reminded;
  Life is short, even at best.
But we have no cause for fearing
  If heaven will be our address.

# TODAY

Time is irretrievable
   It's always moving on.
When today is finished,
   It is forever gone.

The past is just a memory;
   The future a blank page.
Our time ahead indefinite
   Regardless of our age.

Today is all we're given;
   Though we like to plan ahead.
Tomorrow is unknown;
   Let's enjoy today instead.

America

# OUR FLAG

The American flag unifies us;
  portraying our history, our past.
Our flag going into each conflict
  and anchored on battleships' masts.

Our flag represented our country;
  thirteen states becoming a nation.
Red and white stripes, white stars on blue;
  designating a new constellation.

The thirteen stripes have been constant;
  fifty stars now, one for each state.
Over two hundred years in existence
  but our flag is still up-to-date.

Red is a symbol of valor;
  white represents pure and true.
Blue is a symbol of justice;
  perseverance to see the task through.

Our flag portrays our freedom;
  the liberty that we enjoy.
A bond that draws us together;
  the enemies can not destroy.

In battles for freedom from England
  our flag led with drum and with fife.
Minutemen and local militia
  prepared to sacrifice life.

When World Wars enveloped the planet,
  our young men accepted the call.
Troop ships departed for Europe.
  In foreign lands many would fall.

Our flag has been raised on mountains;
  on islands with beaches of sand
Through jungles our brave troops have battled
  to conquer an enemy land.

Our airplanes have flown many missions;
  approaching through hostile terrain;
Dropping their bombs on the targets
  while shrapnel is falling like rain.

Our ships may blockade a harbor;
  strafe beaches before the troops land.
Our ships are a home base for bombers,
  an outpost, a naval command.

Our submarines gliding 'neath oceans;
  through waters so dark and so deep
Are prepared to launch their torpedoes
  while most stringent silence they keep.

We have satellites boosted to orbit
  with cameras to search and to scan;
Technology serving a purpose;
  helping strategists work out a plan.

The flag has been spit on and slandered;
  even burned or worn as a shawl
By dissidents in their rebellion
  who would choose for our country to fall.

Such behavior pains a true patriot
  who salutes as the flag comes in view;
Who believes in the might of our country
  and the wonderful things we can do.

The American flag was launched into space;
  then left on the moon as a token;
A reminder of outreach beyond this earth
  and the memorable words that were spoken.

"ONE SMALL STEP FOR MAN
ONE GIANT LEAP FOR MANKIND"

We pledge our allegiance to the American flag
  and the values for which it stands.
We risk our lives to defend it
  when the world situation demands.

Our flag is placed on the coffin
  of a soldier who died in the fray.
Mere words can't express the emotion
  to convey all we're wanting to say.

Each fold of the flag takes precision;
  each line drawn tight, corners square.
It's a tribute to our fallen heroes
  and a challenge to do and to dare.

The flag, a most precious symbol,
to the family a tangible gift;
At the death of a soldier or sailor
  to honor, esteem and uplift.

The flag is a cover of glory
  for bravery that overcomes fears;
By a country that thanks and remembers
  and honors its fallen through tears.

# PROUD TO BE AN AMERICAN

I'm proud to be an American;
  I'm part of a long, long line.
Washington, Lincoln, Roosevelt
  With citizenship same as mine.

America was founded with lofty ideals
  Of the inherent value of man.
Life, liberty and pursuit of one's dream
  To achieve and be all that one can.

Equality for all the people;
  Laws to treat all folks the same;
Unalienable rights for all mankind;
  Freedoms that each one can claim.

America has resources and riches;
  In so many ways we are blessed.
Opportunities beckon for all who will dare
  As we go forth on our earthly quest.

I'm proud of the wary we are governed;
  By voting we each have a voice.
The losers, or course, are unhappy
  But they follow the majority's choice.

The Navy, Marines, Army, Air Force
  In conflicts have taken a stand;
Defenders of honor and justice
  The heroes of this noble land.

I'm proud to be an American
  With races and cultures so varied;
But when our country is under attack
  As a unit the battle flag's carried.

# ABRAHAM LINCOLN

Adopted son of Illinois;
  Dwelt in Indiana as a boy.

Self-educated, seeking knowledge;
  In frontier days there was no college.

Raised on a farm, much manual labor;
  Always there to help a neighbor.

Plowing, planting, splitting rails;
  With a sense of humor for folksy tales.

Poling a raft to New Orleans;
  He was amazed as he viewed strange scenes.

Cargo ships tied to the dock;
  Black people sold on an auction block.

He read the law, the passed the bar.
  Rode a circuit, near and far.

Married, bought a Springfield house;
  Fathered four sons with his loving spouse.

He had political aspirations;
  The nation was split with great frustrations.

North and South, each chose its route.
  Abe said, "The Union is what it's about."

The presidency was his goal;
  He strove to keep the country whole.

From Illinois he took his leave;
  The highest office to receive.

He led the country, torn by war.
  Year by year, he suffered more.

With battles lost and young men dying
  His very heart and soul were crying.

But he stood firm; wrote a decree
  That all the black folks would be free.

Through grief and pain he pursued the right
  And the Union held at the end of the fight.

He looked ahead to a brighter day
  But he was shot, while attending a play.

In death his worth and value grew
  For surely all the people knew

He gave his all for this great nation.
  Recalled his words at Springfield station;

Before he boarded the east bound train.
  "I know not when I'll return again."

His body was carried to his home state;
  To die for his country had been his fate.

Entombed in Springfield, he had returned.
  Since then, school children have often learned

Of the common man prepared to lead;
  And help this nation to succeed.

A hometown boy, Illinois' own son,
  Returned to his state when the war had been won.

He deserves our gratitude and praise,
  Respect and honor for countless days.

# TRUE FREEDOM

What brings church and state together?
  Equal freedom for mankind.
Free to think and speak our conscience;
  Free to seek the truth to find.

Free to worship as each wishes;
  Serving God as we may choose.
Volunteers to fight for freedom
  With the chance our lives we'll lose.

Rejoicing in our freedom
  Enough to take control;
To discipline our life style
  And let God's power make us whole.

As we value our own freedom.
  Others need their freedom too.
It's not our place to censor --
  Customs, habits, things they do.

By the democratic process;
  Though governed, we're still free.
We are free to vote our conscience;
  We're allowed to disagree.

# A MILITARY LIFE

A military family is different, quite unique.
  My husband served for eighteen years; I know of what I speak.

When he finished high school, he enlisted right away.
  He left for basic training, on the twenty-ninth of May.

We married in the autumn, while he was still in training.
  We lived in basements, one-room flats,
  while knowledge he was gaining.

We had our dreams, our hopes, our plans; we took things in our stride.
  When the troops passed in review, my heart was filled with pride.

Our first permanent assignment was a base in Northern Maine.
  Surrounded by potato fields, three years in harsh terrain.

He re-enlisted for the perks, transfer to warmer weather;
  A larger trailer, a baby girl, the three of us together.

Just six months in the odyssey, his next assignment came.
  A base near the North Pole; Thule, Greenland was its name.

Six months without a sunrise, always dark with wind and snow.
  But that's the military life, you suck it up and go.

A short stretch in Missouri, then selection for Officers' training.
  A difficult transition, but advancement we'd be gaining.

Six months of rigorous training, to honor our country's traditions;
  Preparing to follow commands, in dangerous, adverse conditions.

Graduating as second lieutenants, many had wives in the stands;
  Determined to back up their husbands,
  acquiescing to Air Force demands.

Our next move was South Dakota, with our daughter and infant son.
  My husband took college classes at night after his day's work was done.

Six months TDY to Nebraska, to study, complete his degree.
  I had typed, proof-read many papers; it was also a triumph for me.

The Vietnam war was soon raging; all were needed career soldiers knew.
  My husband was stationed in Thailand, a site from which bombers flew.

Stateside I cared for our children, and delivered our second son;
  I kept busy and cheerful, counting down each day one by one.

His year of duty completed; his return was on Christmas day.
  Next base would be in Oregon, and we were soon on our way.

Being a missile launch officer was an upcoming career
  My husband got into the program; beginning his training that year.

He trained at different locations; just a few months at each base.
  We observed some missile launches, seeing them lift into space.

We were back in government quarters;
he would soon be assigned to a crew.
  Just when life seemed the brightest, all of our future fell through.

Our beautiful ten-year-old daughter, was killed in a crash near the base.
  Three other girls and the driver, were victims at the same place.

Our whole base was affected, five families shocked and in grief.
  Over time all were transferred,
  new surroundings might bring some relief.

Our transfer was to Indiana; Grissom was the base name.
  I slowly rallied and functioned, but my life was never the same.

Two years and then an assignment, the first overseas one for me.
   Ruislip and Wycombe near London; there was much history to see.

Two years and then on to Europe; in Germany we would reside.
   After left-sided driving in England, Autobahns were speedy and wide.

We camped all over the continent; a family adventure for us.
   From Spain to the top of Denmark, crammed in our Volkswagen bus.

My husband had a knee injury; playing squash, running into a wall.
   When he was plagued with arthritis, he scarcely could hobble at all.

Civilian life was now looming; this phase of our life at an end.
   Eighteen years of following orders; to obey, protect, and defend.

So many things had happened, nineteen fifty-five to seventy-three;
   Pages of history were written, and some had even touched me.

I recall the Suez Canal Crisis, and Cuba's Bay of Pigs Invasion;
   The Soviet threat, the Berlin Wall, alerts for a long duration.

The Cuban Missile Crisis and the president's assassination;
   Events of such magnitude; they stunned the entire nation.

The voting rights demonstrations; integration of the schools;
   Non-violent, peaceful protests, became efficient tools.

The lengthy war in Vietnam, a stalemate not a win;
   Requiring such a sacrifice, from America's fighting men.

The hippies and the drop-outs, the "make love, not war" faction
   Encouraged civil protests, to express dissatisfaction.

The space race was a challenge; astronauts a daring breed.
  We committed to the program, that our country might succeed.

John Glenn made first orbits; with each flight men's knowledge grew.
  "Man on the Moon," the mission our country pledged to do.

The countdown, then the liftoff; all systems A-OK.
  In July nineteen sixty-nine, moon mission on its way.

The mission was successful; safe moon landing and return.
  As technology advances, there is so much yet to learn.

Life as a dependent, opened up the world to me.
  A hands-on education; first-hand knowledge; no degree.

Meeting people in their home lands; individuals, not a race.
  Expanding my horizons, while conversing face to face.

Many years have come and gone; I've been a serviceman's mother.
  My sons leaving home at seventeen, was a heartache like no other.

Both went to service academies; one put in a full twenty years.
  I was proud of what they accomplished;
  but for them I shed many tears.

Fifty years of commitment; from my three men folk combined.
  By this lengthy period of service; my lifetime has been defined.

When I hear a salute to our veterans;
each branch recognized with its song
  I'm proud of my family's service; representing our country so long.

# APOLLO 11 LUNAR LANDING
*July 20, 1969*

A milestone for mankind
  Was the journey to the moon.
From earth we watched the LM's descent;
  Our flag was planted soon.

It's been a quarter century
  Since that trip through space by man.
God allowed this lunar conquest;
  Man's dominion was His plan.

God has given man permission
  To maintain, subdue the world.
A challenge was accomplished
  When we saw our flag unfurled.

Though we take pride in our nation
  And the goals which we have met,
God led and blessed that mission
  And He'll be our pilot yet.

We are filled with awe and wonder
  At the scenes from outer space.
It's beyond our comprehension;
  Such a vast and empty place.

By God it was created --
  Same as earth on which we dwell.
The universe is wondrous;
  God doeth all things well!

# THE LIFE OF A SOLDIER

War is declared by Congress
  And announced all over the land.
From the cities to smallest of hamlets,
  Able bodies are soon in demand.

The call goes out for enlistees;
  Volunteers preparing to fight.
Basic training turns boys into soldiers;
  Kids changing to men overnight.

Their uniforms are impressive;
  Bands play as they march in parades.
But war will be so much different,
  Armed combat or going on raids.

Away from home and its comfort;
  All that's familiar and dear.
Dangers lurking where unexpected;
  There is always something to fear!

A buddy becomes all-important;
  Someone on whom to depend.
A comrade through all of the trials
  Till this armed conflict will end.

A friend in all situations;
  Who is always guarding one's back.
When weary, depressed or discouraged,
  He will help you to get back on track.

A buddy serves so many function
  When home seems ever so far.
Drawn closer than to one's own brother;
  Just accepting the way that things are.

Buddies are there for each other;
  Bring cheer when spirits are low.
Share memories of pets, sports and girl-friends
  And the Snack Shack where all the kids go.

Death always lurks in the background
  And luck plays such a large part.
A prayer whether silent or uttered
  Gives courage when skirmishes start.

Troops stand guard for each other;
  Protecting the life of a friend.
In times of danger in combat
  Their lives on each other depend.

Regardless of culture or background
  Soldiers bond to accomplish the goal.
Working to form a strong unit,
  Each ready to fulfill his role.

War levels the landscape;
  Each soldier learns to obey
As they focus on fighting the battle
  While praying they'll be home some day.

# SOMALIA -
## THEY CAME TO FEED THE CHILDREN

They came to feed the children
  With compassion for their need.
But our troops were killed by warlords
  Motivated by their greed.

It seemed a worthy mission
  Till men began to die.
The politicians argued
  While wives and mothers cry.

The brass may count the numbers;
  Say the casualties are few.
But for every fallen soldier
  Dreams and hopes of life are through.

They came to feed the children
  And were murdered in their prime.
Even though they served as soldiers,
  Is their death no less a crime?

The tribal faction leaders
  Whose concerns are power and wealth
Have no respect for human life;
  Regard for children's health.

Dying for their country;
  Sacrifices men will make.
In our grief and pain, we're asking
  Was Somalia a mistake?

# HONORING OUR SOLDIERS

We've become a privileged people;
  Always asking, "what's in it for me?"
But let's remember the soldiers
  Who have fought to keep our country free.

Enlisting or drafted to service;
  Training to further our cause;
Protecting the weak and down-trodden;
  Upholding our standards and laws.

From the days of our revolution
  When Minutemen first took a stand,
Through multiple conflicts and battles
  Our troops have protected our land.

We've fought to support other countries;
  To assist the weak and oppressed.
God has protected our nation;
  By His gracious hand we've been blessed.

This is a time to remember
  Sacrifices that others have made.
Soldiers have suffered their lifetime
  From injuries they have received.

All citizens pledge their commitment;
  Standing tall when the flag's on review.
But the sacrifice made by our soldiers
  Is required of only a few.

Only a small percentage
  Respond to our country's call.
Let's show them respect for their service;
  Providing protection for all.

# NINE-ONE-ONE

Nine-one-one is the number we call
  For assistance when we are distressed;
Auto accidents, heart attacks, strokes, and fires
  Situations that are often addressed.

Nine-one-one is also a date,
  September eleventh each year.
In two thousand one, blind-sided;
  We saw New York's Twin Towers disappear.

We still have many memories
  How we heard of the heinous event.
Who was attacking our country?
  We heard questions wherever we went.

A day of so many emotions;
  Anxiety, fearfulness, pain.
Sorrow for so many losses;
  Thoughts overloading our brain.

We could have never imagined
  Such a bold audacious attack.
Hoodwinked by those living among us
  It was like a sharp stab in the back.

As we watched both towers crumble,
  In a short span of time, all was changed.
The landscape forever altered
  By men who were surely deranged.

The towers were filled with heroes;
  Policemen and firemen who died.
Common people helping each other;
  Volunteering to lead and to guide.

The Pentagon, also a target,
  Was damaged and more lives were lost.
Because of our trusting nature,
  Betrayal at such a great cost.

Another attack plane was thwarted
  Because of a courageous few.
Some passengers caused its destruction.
  Such an unselfish, brave thing to do.

The president went into hiding;
  Air traffic was grounded that day.
Speculations and rumors were common
  And many suggested "Let's pray."

Our government rose to the challenge.
  For once, congress chose to agree.
Affirming our country is Christian
  And praying it shall remain free.

Ten years since all of this happened;
  It is fitting that each should remember
How Americans rallied to our country's support
  That eleventh day of September.

# HONORING OUR VETERANS

A day to honor veterans;
  To show appreciation
For those who answered duty's call
  To serve, protect our nation.

Through succeeding generations
  Men responded to the call;
To do battle for our homeland;
  Give protection for us all.

Many lost their lives in combat;
  Far from all they held most dear.
We pause to pay them homage
  On Veteran's Day each year.

Many more have scars from injuries
  Both to body and to brain.
The flashbacks of traumatic times
  Cause years of lingering pain.

Young folks are patriotic;
  They enlist to fill a need.
They train, become a unit;
  Follow as the sergeants lead.

Wars seem never-ending;
  The world has much unrest;
But when we aid our allies
  We send our country's best.

Today we still have veterans
  Who fought in World War Two,
Korea, Viet Nam, Kuwait.
  Some strangers, some we knew.

These men of different ages
  All at one time in their prime;
Now deserve some recognition;
  We can thank them any time.

They sacrificed for country
  And managed to survive;
Let's give each one respect they're due
  As long as they're alive.

# TRUE PATRIOTISM

Our hearts may swell when we see the flag;
  We stand at attention as it passes by.
We are ready to pledge our allegiance;
  But let other be injured or die.

We are not touched in a personal way;
  We continue our normal routine.
We are willing to act patriotic
  To fit the appropriate scene.

To serve in our country's Armed Forces
  A career choice we think is just fine.
We say it's great for young people;
  But just if they're no kin of mine.

Soldiers killed in terrorist battles
  Are brought home to their resting place.
Terminology that is media friendly;
  But they're dead and the grave is their space.

Making speeches, waving flags, blowing trumpets
  In no way can ever compare
To the sacrifice of the fallen,
  The American kids who were there.

A service commitment is voluntary;
  But who are the ones that will go?
The young seeking means of advancement;
  The horrors of war they don't know.

The burden is carried by only a few.
  The percentage of soldiers is small.
There's no way to ever repay them
  As they sacrifice for us all.

America is a great country;
  A homeland that immigrants crave;
But the warriors going forth into battle
  Are the youth who are naive and brave.

The rhetoric comes from the leaders;
  But others must fight for their plan.
Let's honor our troops, the real heroes
  In all of the ways that we can.

# ARE WE A NATION UNDER GOD?

Are we a nation under God
  Or have we gone astray?
Are we too proud, self-satisfied,
  And doing things our way?

We may not worship idols
  Of stone, or glass, or clay;
But we sell out for comforts
  And possessions every day.

Our yearnings for the good life
  Lead to working for more pay.
Overtime upon the job;
  No time for God today!

We need to turn from earthly aims
  And chart a course that's new;
Return to values of the past;
  Ask God what we should do.

Sin's pleasures do not ever last;
  God's blessings are life-long.
God wants to guide our nation
  If we'll turn from sin and wrong.

Love

# GOD IS LOVE!
### *(1 John 4: 16-19)*

God is love!
  A love that's so surprising.
Giving what we don't deserve,
  Such love is mesmerizing.

A love that overfloweth
  To touch each living being.
Man is given hope and mercy;
  Through creation, God's love seeing.

A love that knows no limit;
  Dispensed without a fee.
No price is placed upon it;
  God's love is always free.

A love of such dimension
  Because God is pure love.
Love is poured upon us
  Like raindrops from above.

God is love!
  A love that seeks each soul.
In sin, despair or darkness
  His love can make us whole.

God is love!
  A love that is not priced.
We need not trade or barter;
  He gives new life in Christ.

God is love!
  A love that fails us never.
Sustaining through our daily trials,
  A love that is forever.

God is love!
  So how should we respond?
Share His love with those around us
  And with all the world beyond.

# TRUE LOVE

How often do we pause to think what true love really means?
Too often we associate true love with movie scenes.
The room is softly lighted; background music sets the tone.
There are no noisy children or the shrill of telephone.

The table is set with china and the candles have been lit.
No one is late for dinner; working overtime a bit.
Such romantic love is special like a childhood fairy tale;
But without a deeper focus such love is prone to fail.

True love includes the bad times with the colds and stomach flu;
Sleepless nights with crying babies; days of unemployment too.
At the fanciest of weddings older women often cry.
They know hardships are looming; it's a fact one can't deny.

Couples need long-term commitment; be prepared to see it through.
Couples loyal to each other and to their children too.
True love meets disappointments and accepts what can't be altered;
With mates who hold each other up when one of them has faltered.

Love is built on more than daydreams; it's a covenant to share.
With God as head of household and a time of daily prayer.
True love is not a Valentine; it is day-by-day behavior.
With love for family, fellow man and Jesus Christ the Savior.

# IN MARRIAGE

A man shall cleave unto his wife;
  The two as one become.
A commandment straight from God
  For all, not just for some.

With space as individuals,
  Like two branches of a tree
Growing from a sturdy trunk
  Attached, yet somewhat free.

Concerned for each one's welfare;
  As a unit setting goals;
Adjusting with time's passage
  To life's changes and new roles.

Always clinging to God's promise
  That all things will work for good;
Trusting God to bless the marriage,
  It will turn out as it should.

# THE DUMPSTER

So much of life in a dumpster;
  The hopes, the sorrows, the joys;
Everything from one's wedding dress
  To the kids once treasured toys.

A chapter of life has now ended
  But not by one's choice or decision.
When a spouse decides he is leaving,
  He no longer listens to reason.

He walks out on all his commitments;
  Away from the daily routine.
He's ready for freedom from family;
  Reverts to the bachelor scene.

It lowers the standard of living;
  A mortgage is still to be paid.
A woman with only her children,
  At night so alone and afraid.

A lengthy time of transition,
  Divorcing and starting anew;
A move to a nearby apartment;
  Less rooms and the closets are few.

A dumpster is the solution,
  Fill it with dreams from the past;
But even without all the objects
  The memories are destined to last.

# PLEASURES, POSSESSIONS, POSITION

The lures of the world are enticing;
  Men lust for so many things.
It is a part of their nature
  From beggars to rich men to kings.

So often the goal is for pleasure;
  More leisure, fine dining, new clothes.
Pleasure is not true fulfillment;
  So often it is only a pose.

If the goal is possessions,
  There's always desires to have more.
Things that are bigger and better
  And stuff on display in the store.

Men often strive for position,
  Prestige, recognition and fame,
Admired, respected and famous;
  The object of worldly acclaim.

Pleasure, possessions, positions
  Will never fulfill all our dreams.
Life is so empty and aimless;
  No reason for living it seems.

Love is the reason for living.
  God loves us and we can respond;
Loving and trusting Him fully
  In this life and in time beyond.

Our life can be a reflection
  Of God's timeless and wonderful love.
We reveal it in treatment of others
  And respect for our Father above.

# HURT IN THE FAMILY

Hurt in the family cannot be resolved

   Till we consciously plan to forgive.

Till we take the first step of the process,

   In a prison of anguish we'll live.


Forgiveness leads us to ponder

   And accept the blame we must share.

To face just how much we are hurting;

   How burdened with pain and despair.


In forgiveness we let go of anger.

   Work it through; let it dissolve.

Close the door; quit dwelling upon it;

   With courage, forgive and absolve.


Security in Christ the Savior

   Gives us strength to set others free.

By forgiving past indiscretions,

   Just as Christ forgave you and me.

# SECOND OPPORTUNITIES

Second opportunities
  Don't always come our way.
A chance for new beginnings
  When we have gone astray.

A chance to rectify our past;
  To overcome our failing.
Our sinful misdeeds blotted out;
  No more behind us trailing.

Second chances may not come
  From government or mate.
One failure and we're written off;
  For us it is too late.

But God gives second chances
  In a personal, private way.
Jesus meets us one by one
  And our sins on Him we lay.

Jesus tells us to start over;
  Follow him and get it right.
Just follow in His footsteps;
  Always keep Him in our sight.

# TOUGH LOVE

When we first see our babies,
  We want to keep them near;
Protect them, hold and shield them
  From so many things we fear.

Tough love is part of mothering;
  We have to let them grow.
They crawl, then soon are walking;
  There are always falls we know.

Tough love is many other things
  A mom's required to do
Like taking kids for routine shots
  And having teeth filled too.

Tough love is really needed
  When off to school they go.
Mom feels so sad and lonely
  But she doesn't let them know.

Tough love is gentle prodding
  When the task ahead is tough.
Mom counsels you will conquer
  If you just persist enough.

Tough love gives children options;
  Gradually lets them take control.
As they learn to make good choices,
  Independence is the goal.

# BEING A GRANDMOTHER

Did Jesus have a grandma?
  Was He part of a big clan?
Did His grandma watch Him grow
  From a boy into a man?

Was extended family waiting
  For Egyptian trip to end?
Was there family still in Nazareth
  On whom Joseph could depend?

Had Mary missed her mother?
  Was there lots of news to share?
Did His grandma have an inkling
  Of the Cross which Christ would bear?

Were there family get-togethers?
  Did His grandma cook and bake?
Did Jesus have a favorite food;
  Dates, figs, or honey cake?

Did Grandma stitch a sturdy robe
  And weave a little belt?
When she saw Jesus wear it,
  Imagine how she felt.

With a grandson in my family
  How can I not relate
To Jesus's earthly family
  And their joy which was so great.

If Jesus had a grandma
  Did she feel just like me
When she gave Him hugs and kisses
  And she bounced Him on her knee?

As Jesus dwelt with family
   Imagine how they shared
Joy in His growth and training
   As for manhood He prepared.

I'm blessed with a baby grandson
   To enjoy, and help to train
I'm praying God will lead him
   Through life's problems, hurts, and pain.

He's so small and sweet and precious
   But with time he'll change and grow;
And because I love him dearly
   I'll release him, watch him go.

A grandma's role is special
   To accept, to love, to praise;
To listen and encourage
   Through all of childhood days.

From the days of Baby Jesus
   To the infants born today,
Grandmas take a lot of pleasure
   When grandkids they display.

My grandson is a blessing
   On the future I'll not dwell;
Since Jesus lived and died for us
   I'll trust that all is well.

# GOD'S LOVE

Nothing is able to cancel
　The love of God from our life.
His love cannot be severed
　By razor, by sword, or by knife.

God's love is ever enduring;
　Sustaining, whatever befall.
When life seems utterly hopeless,
　He comforts when on Him we call.

God's love helps us to conquer
　Because we can trust and depend
On God's presence beside us
　Till death brings our life to an end.

Nothing can separate us
　From the love God will provide.
Whatever our dire situation,
　He surely will be by our side.

# Family

# A MARRIAGE PATCHWORK QUILT

A marriage resembles a patchwork quilt;
   Each partner brings scraps from the past.
By choosing the best of the fabric
   A union is built that will last.

Love is required for the backing
   To which the quilt top is fused;
A beautiful life is created
   When only choice fabrics are used.

A lining of cheer and good humor
   Makes it easy to start each new day.
With faith to join it together,
   The stitches are anchored to stay.

With time the colors will mellow;
   Individual pieces may fade.
Desires and goals will be blended
   As lifetime commitments are made.

From such a jumbled beginning
   A pattern for life will appear.
With compromise by each partner
   The marriage improves year by year.

# MOTHERHOOD -
# A UNIVERSAL CALLING

Women have been mothers
  Since the world began,
Caring for their children
  According to God's plan.

Their cultures may be different
  And their language different too.
But Mothers are so much alike
  In things they say and do.

In caring for their children
  And providing for their needs;
In teaching them the way that's right
  And praising their good deeds.

Women who are mothers
  Are all very much the same;
Wanting good things for their children
  More than power or wealth or fame.

# A FATHER

What is the task of a father?
  To discipline, encourage, and teach;
To set the child an example;
  Set goals for the child to reach.

Be aware that each child is different
  With traits that are his alone.
Discipline firmly but wisely;
  Each child has needs of his own.

Encourage the child to feel worthy,
  Self-confident, poised and secure;
Able to meet life's temptations;
  Not tempted by worldly allure.

Instruct by setting up guidelines;
  Explain the reasons for rules;
That wisdom comes through learning
  And ignorance is the province of fools.

Unconditional love from their parents
  Is a gift each child should receive.
Spiritual gifts are important
  So the child can know Christ and believe.

# A BABY GIRL

A Baby is always special;
  But more so if it is your own.
How could such utter perfection
  Be found in one baby alone?

Surrounded by love and affection,
  She's the answer to Mom and Dad's dream.
As they welcome her into the family,
  She is part of each plan or each scheme.

A tiny seven pound treasure;
  Whether awake or asleep.
Everything about her is special;
  A baby is precious, unique.

Two people can be a family
  But it's even more fun when there's three.
As you cherish your little daughter,
  How great the future will be.

# MY DAUGHTER

Vicki Jo Alumbaugh (1957 - 1968)


Mother's Day is very hard
  For anyone like me.
It causes me to stop and think
  How I wish things could be.


It calls to my awareness
  Just how much I have lost,
A daughter taken from me
  At such tremendous cost.


A child no longer with me;
  A daughter that's no more.
An end to many hopes and dreams
  Like closing of a door.


With time the pain has faded
  But the memories still are clear;
And in my imagination
  She's thirty-one this year.


I imagine her achievements
  And the start of her career.
And think she could have married
  And my grandkids might be here.

At a Mother-Daughter Banquet
  I see families filled with pride;
And I could be just like them
  If my daughter had not died.

I'm humbled by experience
  I'm tempered by the pain.
My heart was softened by the tears
  As fields soaked by rain.

Now I search more for blessings;
  I'm more thankful when I pray.
Loss has changed my values;
  I live from day to day.

I know she was a Christian
  And I'll see her by and by
But at Mother-Daughter Banquets
  Excuse me if I cry.

# TO FILL THE ROLE OF MOTHERS

A mother's love is special;
  Mothers nourish, nurture, train.
A mother's love is constant
  When her children cause her pain.

A mother's love is timeless;
  She has so much to recall.
From infancy through childhood,
  She has memories of it all.

A mother's love is helpful;
  When she's needed, she is there.
A Christian mom seeks guidance
  As she turns to God in prayer.

Motherhood's a special calling
  To perpetuate the race.
Through succeeding generations
  There are trials mothers face.

A mother's job description
  Lists so many things to do.
Each mom has different talents;
  They need help from others too.

Women fill the role of mothers
  When they help a child in need.
When they tutor or encourage
  And they help a child succeed.

Women fill the role of mothers
  As a very special friend
When teens need more than family
  On whom they can depend.

Women fill the role of mothers
  Perhaps, even unaware.
They are honorary mothers;
  When needed they are there.

We thank God for all women
  Who fulfill a mother's role.
Helping children grow and function
  Is a truly worthy goal.

# MOTHERHOOD (CONNECTED)

The babe which nestled 'neath your heart
  Now is on its own;
But it will still be in your heart
  Even when it's grown.

It's yours for just a few short years
  To teach, to train, to mold.
Then one day in surprise you'll ask,
  "When did you get so old?"

You were connected by a cord;
  At birth the cord was broken.
But still you'll share a special bond,
  Invisible, unspoken.

# A MOTHER'S HANDS

With all the thought and emphasis
　On perpetrating youth,
We cannot stop the march of time
　For hands reveal the truth.

For hands are illustrations
　Of the toil  throughout one's life.
The cleaning, scrubbing, laundry
　Routine duties of a wife.

The mowing, planting, digging
　To beautify the yard.
Sanding, painting, waxing,
　On hands, these jobs are hard.

Such hands have spots and wrinkles;
　And the skin is coarse and rough.
The youthful look can't be restored;
　No lotion is enough.

In older life those work-worn hands
　Reveal their toil for others.
The routine chores all done in love;
　The tasks of wives and mothers.

Such hands are illustrations
　That a family's needs were met.
Though wrinkled, rough or knobby,
　There is beauty in them yet.

# MY MOM
### "Ruby Grace Walden Blair"

I knew my mom of ninety-five years
  For quite a lot of that time.
We've been in some valleys together
  And we've had some mountains to climb.

I knew her first as caregiver;
  When a baby, she watched over me.
I knew her also as my teacher
  When she read as I sat on her knee.

I knew her as thrifty, hard-working
  With so many farm chores to do.
The highlight each evening was supper
  After all of the day's work was through.

I knew her as cheerful and giving;
  Always ready to lend or to share.
She saw and met needs of our neighbors;
  Whether bread or a warm coat to wear.

I knew her as gracious and friendly;
  Always ready to set out a meal.
Killing a chicken and cooking from scratch
  To her was routine, no big deal.

I knew her as fun-loving, quirky;
  April Fool's Day was time for some scheme.
We would fall for some far-fetched story
  And then "April Fool" she would scream.

I knew her as firm and determined
  She said, "You will all get through school.
No dropouts, no weddings, no possible cause."
  She said it, so that was the rule.

I knew her as stout-hearted, tender;
  She saw me through days that were tough.
As an Air Force wife and a mother,
  I experienced times that were rough.

I knew her as suffering, heart-broken
  When her grandchild, my daughter, died.
We were joined in our pain and our anguish;
  Precious memories we shared as we cried.

I knew her as patient, accepting
  When through death Dad was taken away.
She accepted her role as a widow
  As God walked beside her each day.

I knew her as grand-children's idol;
  She was truly respected, admired.
She attended school functions and weddings
  And was always neatly attired.

I knew her as health gradually faded;
  Weakened limbs till she could not walk.
But she testified of her Savior
  As long as she managed to talk.

I knew her as a role model;
  An example of how we should live.
Encouragement, praise or instruction;
  She always had something to give.

I knew her as a long-term Christian,
  In all ways reflecting God's light;
Always ready to praise and to serve Him;
  Walking in faith, not by sight.

Christ's in our hearts, not a building;
  But the cross on this church is aglow.
Reminder of past; hope of future
  For family and friends left below.

Christ's light overcomes the darkness;
  It cleanses and covers our sin.
When we come to the cross for forgiveness,
  Our new life in Christ can begin.

For her family Mom led by example
  And the light of her love lingers on.
She can still be our example
  Though from this world she is gone.

# MOTHERHOOD

Although we think we are ready,
  For motherhood, we're not prepared.
A helpless baby is placed in our arms
  And we are humbled and scared.

This child on us is dependent
  For all of its nurture and care.
Whenever our baby has issues,
  Will we sense its need and be there?

The first year, a time of such progress,
  First word, Is it "mama" or "dad?"
Crawling, standing, then walking,
  Where is the infant we had?

A toddler is always exploring
  But Mom is his mentor, his guide.
He's cautious of play dates with others;
  Reassured, if Mom's by his side.

Beginning of school is a passage
  From the home to a world that is wide.
Attempting new things, winning, losing,
  Mom is just proud if he tried.

The years so quickly keep passing;
  There's a teenager learning to drive.
Their license gives them more freedom;
  Independence for which all youth strive.

Graduation - the end of an era;
  The days of his childhood are gone.

But heartfelt prayers of his mother
  For this child will go on and on.

The ceaseless love of a mother
  Is a constant on which one depends;
As their relationship deepens,
  Two adults become bonded as friends.

Relationships will keep changing
  As parents and children both age;
But the steadfast love of a mother
  May be sensed by her child at each stage.

There's a pleasure in talking with mother;
  A phone call to brighten her day.
Just the joy of being remembered
  By a child who lives far away.

Mom is sometimes taken for granted;
  Of her needs we may be unaware.
Small gestures can be so important;
  Little tokens that show her we care.

Regardless our age, we're an orphan;
  When Mom dies, we're on our own.
But her words still echo around us,
  "With God, you're never alone!"

Assuming the role of a mother
  And doing the best that one can;
Rearing a Christ-centered family
  For a woman is God's chosen plan.

# MY DAD

## "Paul Wendell Blair"

Ten years have passed since Daddy died;
  The memories grow more dim.
But still I see him mowing lawns;
  An old man, tanned and slim.

My father worked to raise us right,
  Six daughters and a son.
He taught us to stick with a job
  Until the task was done.

Although he had four daughters first,
  He didn't seem to care.
"Sure you can do it, Sister!"
  Was the message he would share.

He never showed emotions much;
  His love was not expressed.
But still he took such pride in us;
  His family was the best.

That year when he was very ill
  His daughters all were there.
Through restless days or sleepless nights,
  We gave him loving care.

Sometimes he didn't know us;
  His thoughts were in the past.
As he recalled his lifetime,
  It all went by so fast.

And then there were the good times
  When he knew us all by name.
When it was time for us to leave
  He'd thank us that we came.

One day a nurse came bustling in
  And standing by his bed
Asked, "Anything you need today?"
  "More girls" was all he said.

# MY BLESSINGS

I am surrounded by blessing;
  As abundant as snowflakes or rain.
God gives me His strength and His comfort
  When I'm in trouble or pain.

Blessing for day-to-day living
  Remind of God's goodness to me.
I gaze from my living room window
  And God's changing landscape I see.

Through the annual cycle of season
  Each year there's a time of rebirth.
I'm blessed by God's revelation
  That He's in control of this earth.

God has blessed me as I'm growing older;
  He helps me to trust, not to doubt.
He has blessed me with more understanding
  Of my purpose and what life's about.

I've always been a caregiver
  With six siblings younger than me;
Then nurturing my own three children
  Wherever we happened to be.

Through the sudden death of my daughter,
  My faith was barely enough.
God gave me the strength to keep going;
  To care for my sons and hang tough.

My sons went to West Point and Air Force;
  A top education that's free;

Survival school and airborne training
  Were difficult phases for me.

I cared for Dad through final illness
  And was there for Mom twenty more years.
I rejoiced when she went to heaven
  Celebrating her demise through my tears.

Last week was my seventy-ninth birthday;
  I'm the eldest of family that's left.
Knowing no one is older to turn to
  I sometimes feel lonely, bereft.

Then I turn to God for assurance
  That He's with me, and will see me through.
I know He will not forsake me
  Whatever I still have to do.

To marriage vows I've been faithful;
  Almost sixty years we've been wed.
Hardships have kept us together;
  Becoming blessings instead!

Earthly time is now fleeting
  So each day I choose to have fun
As I find some special blessing
  Like the rays of the bright morning sun.

A bird on the windowsill, singing
  Or squirrels that frolic and play;
Thank you God for each blessing
  Provided for me day by day.

# REFLECTIONS OF A GRANDMOTHER

My grandchild tugs at the strings of my heart;
  Taps the depths of my love and affection.
Holding a newborn so helpless and small
  Was a time for pensive reflection.

The years slipped away to a time that is past;
  When his parent was placed in my arms.
I see in his son a resemblance
  And I'm captured by all of his charms.

We all are aware we are mortal;
  We are links in life's unending chain.
Through my grandson our line will continue
  And God's love for mankind is plain.

Each day with my grandson is special;
  I watch him progress and grow.
The whole world to him is a mystery
  With new things to see, try and know.

He marvels when fan-blades are turning;
  Sees light fixtures twinkle and shine.
He kicks and he squeals in his bathtub;
  On oatmeal is ready to dine.

He enjoys meeting lots of new people;
  Is quick to gurgle and smile.
As I cuddle him close while he's sleeping,
  I am thankful to hold him awhile.

I'm told about other grandchildren;
  See their pictures; hear what they can do.
But for me this year is special;
  For the role of grandmother is new.

# FRIENDSHIP

Our friendship is too precious
  To let it slip away.
We need to get together;
  Let's find the time some way.

We have so much in common;
  You are my special friend.
You always are so cheerful;
  On your viewpoint I depend.

We share in times of trouble;
  When our spirits need a lift.
We have an understanding
  That is a special gift.

Let's check our daily planners;
  Find a date when we're both free.
Then pencil in a place and time
  To meet, just you and me.

To catch up on the latest news;
  To share our hearts' desires.
To undergird each other
  For whatever life requires.

# A TRUE FRIEND

When someone asks me how I am,
  I always say, "just fine."
I smile and act real happy
  While I quote the standard line.

Contacts are superficial
  With most people whom I meet.
I cannot share my problems
  With everyone I greet.

I hide my disappointments
  And I wear a bright veneer.
I present a smiling image;
  I'm a vision of good cheer.

What lies behind this outer shell?
  Is it failure, loss or pain?
Does anybody care enough
  To let me just complain?

To listen to my problems;
  To see why I am stressed;
To let me share anxieties
  When lonesome and depressed?

I need an empathetic friend
  With willingness to share;
A one-on-one relationship
  That's built on mutual care.

You meet all these requirements;
  Plus you're also lots of fun.
The friend I searched for many years,
  Dear Shirley, you're the one.

## NEW BEGINNINGS

"Every good thing must come to an end"
  Is an adage we've often heard said;
But I choose to think that an ending
  Is a time to accept, not to dread.

From endings, come start-ups, beginnings;
  Adapting to things that are new;
Finding our place in the picture;
  Learning all of the things we can do.

As a child we depend on our mother
  We think she does everything right.
She wakes us for school in the morning
  And tucks us in bed when it's night.

We see her as perfect, all-knowing;
  The one in whom we can trust.
She is able to solve all out problems
  After pros and cons are discussed.

She's there whenever we need her
  Through the difficult years as a teen.
We vary from loving to hateful;
  It seems there is no in-between.

She gives us our independence
  When we move to a place of our own.
Now there is distance between us
  But we always can reach her by phone.

We love her and we respect her
  But we are in no way aware;
The depth of love she has for us
  Until our own baby we bear.

Each birth is a special beginning;
  For the family an awaited event.
A new mother gazes in wonder
  At this child that the Lord to her sent.

Dependent, helpless and needy;
  A baby touches her heart.
The day it enters the family
  A new phase of living will start.

A mother stores up the memories;
  Delights in the growth of her child.
Recalls when so tiny, so precious
  And the very first time that it smiled.

She finds herself being her mother;
  Saying things in the very same way.
Warning what dire things will happen
  If a child chooses not to obey.

Time keeps rushing onward.
  Children grow but grandparents age.
Elderly, growing dependent;
  Life approaching its final stage.

Death, expected or sudden,
  For all of the family a shock.
If death could have been halted,
  We'd have chosen to just stop the clock.

We'd bargain with God for some more time
  If there were a possible chance.
But from birth our days have been numbered
  And toward death each day we advance.

Over time we come to acceptance;
  Remember the closeness, the love.
We look toward that special beginning
  When we join them in Heaven above.

As long as this planet keeps spinning,
  Families upon it will dwell.
With mother, as mother, without her,
  Each role women handle quite well.

There is joy in all of these seasons;
  From youth to the days we are old.
We cannot go back to relive them
  But the memories are precious as gold.

God made provision for families.
  It was part of His eternal plan.
Generations, sharing and bonding,
  Overlapping through years of life span.

# RUBY GRACE

A precious infant - so adored;
  A family name is now restored.
Connection on the family tree;
  What was, what is, and what will be.

Change is a major part of living;
  Yet tradition you are giving.
A name that earned respect and praise
  For a virtuous woman all her days.

You will guide little Ruby as she grows
  But her life's direction no one knows.
Encourage her to do her best
  And trust in God to do the rest.

# AS YOU GRADUATE
### Jacob Todd Alumbaugh - 2013

I'm an old-fashioned Nana
  Expecting your good sense to rule.
You must sacrifice life's little pleasures
  To succeed at a prestigious school.

Being present in all of the classes,
  Taking notes and reading the text,
Working out the difficult problems,
  Prepared for whatever is next.

Looking forward to life and its challenge;
  Seeking ways to excel in your field.
When you chose a bio-med major,
  Your course for the future was sealed.

Ask God to always be with you;
  To direct the plans you pursue.
As a child of His glorious kingdom,
  Give Him praise in all that you do.

Life has its up and down moments;
  Sometimes you will fail to excel.
Through faith in God and endurance
  In time you will surely do well.

As you go off to college,
  Each day I will lift you in prayer
And if you have some nagging problem,
  I will listen if you need to share.

I'm proud that you are my grandson;
  A part of the family I'll leave.
My legacy for future seasons;
  In Christ each professed, and believe.

In some way each person is special'
  I remember when you were small.
Each day you soaked up more knowledge
  And tried to find use for it all.

Always keep that perspective;
  Be open to concepts, though new.
Test theories, be sure they're authentic;
  Let ethics and morals guide you.

You have been loved by your family;
  Your past is a part of the mix.
I pray that the training of Nana
  In your sub-conscious mind always sticks.

# Memories

# THE OLD ROCKING CHAIR

This antique chair was precious
  For my family and me.
As my mom would rock the baby
  We would nestle by her knee.

When we were young and sheltered,
  Safe in the family nest
We dreamed about the future
  When we'd conquer every test.

We had time for songs and stories
  And to share our hopes and dreams.
Mom praised us for our progress
  And encouraged all our schemes.

This chair rocked Grandma's babies
  And Great-grandma used it too.
This was a prized possession
  When furnishings were few.

Great-great-granddad built it
  Moved it on a wagon train
When his family left Ohio
  Never to return again.

This chair holds family history
  Of mothers, one by one,
Caring for their children
  Until their task was done.

Of babies swiftly growing
  Of childhood days soon past.
The child became the mother
  And life went by so fast.

As succeeding generations
  Were nurtured in this chair;
The things our mothers taught us
  Went with us everywhere.

The family as a unit
  Was ordained by Christ our Lord.
When we gathered round the rocker,
  We were all of one accord.

# THE NEW YEAR

A moment in time
  Brings the year to an end
According to the calendar
  On which we depend.

A cycle has ended
  And we're starting anew
So I often make lists
  Of the things I will do.

I make resolutions
  To diet, lose weight
To vacuum and dust;
  Not stay up so late.

Each year I take stock
  Of the things I regret;
Of the things I've accomplished;
  What needs doing yet.

I'm so nostalgic
  As I think of past days;
Of loved ones who've died
  Or have gone other ways.

As I look to the New Year
  And what it will bring;
I'm encouraged to know
  Winter's followed by Spring.

Life's always uncertain;
  There's no guarantee;
But whatever comes
  Jesus Christ is with me.

I ask Him for cleansing
  As a new year begins.
He forgives my past failings;
  He wipes out my sins.

I'll make my best effort
  To serve Him all year;
To meet needs of others;
  To spread love and cheer.

Jesus helps me go forward
  Though the future's unclear.
Through good times and bad times
  I will persevere.

# BIRTHDAY SENTIMENTS

Another Birthday! Can it be?
  How fast the years go by!
We cannot stop the march of time;
  Not even if we try.

Six sisters in our group;
  Each aging more each year;
And for the oldest ones of us
  Retirement age grows near.

But when we get together
  We recall what used to be;
When we broke the handle from the broom
  Or fell out of the cherry tree.

Our favorite recreation
  Is to meet together and chat.
We see ourselves as in our youth
  Not graying, or limping, or fat.

The nicest part of a birthday;
  No matter how old we will get
Is sharing the day together
  And being "THE BLAIR GIRLS" yet.

# OUR ELLIOTT CEMETERY OUTING

Our cemetery outing is a highlight of the year.
  Because of pleasant memories, our loved ones still seem near.

Mom always told of visits to the grave site of her dad.
  This remembrance of their father made his little family glad.

They walked to the graveyard, picked wild flowers along the way;
  Placed a bouquet upon his plot, were proud of their display.

He had no engraved monument, just a rock to mark his space.
  Grandma worked to raise her family, being poor was no disgrace.

Grandma's parents were laid to rest on this cemetery hill
  And over years more family graves the empty plots would fill.

My aunt and then my grandma went to their eternal rest;
  My mom and dad were buried there, it was at their request.

On Memorial weekend Sunday, we always congregate;
  Eleven o'clock the meeting time; some are early, some are late.

We all contribute to a fund for a basket for each space.
  A silk arrangement on a hook is hung by each one's place.

Then we add personal tokens, a peony or a rose.
  Nostalgic thoughts of special times; how fast each lifetime goes.

The cemetery's on a hill; the turn-in sharp and steep.
   It's isolated, calm, remote, where family members sleep.

The early comers wonder, who will the next car be?
   Until it rounds the corner, they can hear it but not see.

We have our own tradition; children rolling down the hill.
   Adults may join the action proving they are youthful still.

Those who marry in our family, roll down the hillside too.
   It's just a rite-of-passage that good sports are glad to do.

We honor by remembrance, share tales of by-gone years;
   Ancestors become real to all, there's laughter more than tears.

We assemble for a picnic lunch; time seems to melt away;
   But we'll get together next year on Memorial week Sunday.

For each our days are limited, just a certain number to fill;
   But we're prepared to meet our Lord,
   leave our bodies on Elliott's Hill.

# A MOTHER'S DAY CARD

A card can never say it all;
  Too many thoughts to share.
But by my daily actions
  I hope you know I care.

You're in my thoughts while jogging
  And I breathe a prayer for you.
I ask for God's protection
  Whatever you may do.

I follow your example
  And the values you believe.
I recall my childhood memories
  And much pleasure I receive.

I'll always try to honor you
  And never cause you pain.
If I don't say "I love you,"
  May my actions make it plain.

# THE SCHOOL BUS

I loved to see the school bus
  As it stopped before our gate.
I was waiting anxiously
  Whenever it was late.

My kids came running up the lane
  With news about the day.
They shared the good and bad with me
  Before they went to play.

My life revolved around their needs;
  The cookies I should bake;
The days of chaperoning
  On field trips they would take.

Helping with their homework;
  Reviewing for a test;
Saying how important
  To always do their best.

Those days are long behind me;
  The school bus stops no more.
Sometimes I see it passing
  If I'm glancing out the door.

My children now are grown.
  I've moved on to other things.
But when I see the bus go by
  What memories it brings.

# CHARLIE

We have a cat named Charlie
  But we just call her Chuck.
    Her tail was amputated
When run over by our truck.

A change of personality
  Resulted from that drama.
    She moved beneath the back porch stoop;
  Avoided all life's trauma.

In a moment of compassion
  I let her move inside;
    And soon this change of status
She was taking right in stride.

She dominates the household;
  Is vocal with demands
    With meows of agitation,
Quick responses she commands.

She meows for our attention
  When her food dish needs refilled,
    When her litter box needs changing,
Or her water pan has spilled.

She always finds a cozy spot
  To stretch out for a nap.
    She lets us stroke her tummy;
But won't perch upon our lap.

She gazes out the windows;
  Never ventures out the door.
    She pretends to have no knowledge
What a scratching post is for.

Her coat is black and glossy;
  Her green eyes are bright and clear
    But her irritating habits
Are what make her seem so dear.

# THE HARVEST

I grew up on a subsistence farm;
  Six sisters and one little brother.
The harvest provided our winter food;
  We learned to rely on each other.


We gathered in onions, potatoes and pumpkins
  Grew popcorn for our nightly treat.
Cracked hickory nuts used for baking;
  Their flavor couldn't be beat.


We canned green beans, peaches and berries
  In quart jars, then stored them away.
Our hens provided us fresh eggs;
  Roast chicken on Thanksgiving Day.


In the first cold snap of winter
  It was time to have some fresh meat.
A neighbor helped us butcher a hog;
  We had pork of all kinds we could eat.


Our cows required milking twice daily;
  We knew each one by her name.
Their milk and cream were delicious;
  Like pets, they were docile and tame.

Cutting trees and filling the wood lot;
  Stacking logs in a pile near the door;
Stockpiling for snow storms and blizzards
  Was what all the planning was for.

We were used to changes in weather;
  The droughts, high winds, heavy rains.
We depended on nature's provision;
  Were thankful for harvest of grain.

Our main crop was corn by the bushel;
  Shucked by hand as it hung on the stalk.
Dad filled the wagon with all of the ears
  While his horses down each row would walk.

Such a life was surely not easy
  But our hard work drew us together.
Dormancy followed the harvest;
  There was less work in inclememt weather.

Technology brought many changes;
  Fresh food is in stores through the year.
But when we relied on the harvest,
  God's presence seemed ever so near.

# THE JACK-O-LANTERNS

A phenomenon this autumn
  Seen almost every place
Is a large, orange, plastic garbage bag
  With a jack-o-lantern face.

The bag is filled with rags or leaves
  From bottom to the top.
If they were really pumpkins,
  We'd have a bumper crop.

One side has a smiling face;
  The other one wears a frown.
According to the owner's mood,
  He can turn the bag around.

Is this just a passing fancy
  Or a continuing trend that will last?
Are plastic bag jack-o-lanterns
  In the permanent Halloween cast?

There's room for innovations
  And technology is great;
But plastic bags cannot supply
  Punkin' pie upon our plate.

# BUSTER

This morning when I got up;  
  My little dog was dead.  
Today my thoughts are in the past,  
  Can't think of times ahead.

A member of our family  
  Sharing with us through the years.  
Now all I have are memories;  
  In my sorrow I shed tears.

When he was just a puppy,  
  At Lake Paradise dumped out;  
Construction workers at the dam  
  Left scraps of food about.

All summer they were busy  
  And he watched them work each day;  
But when the job was finished  
  They packed up and moved away.

The days grew short and cooler  
  And the nights were long and dark.  
In puzzlement he waited  
  Didn't howl or growl or bark.

Each day as I ran past him;  
  For this puppy I felt sad.  
One day I made a return trip;  
  Took dog food that I had.

I opened up the package;  
  Poured out a little mound.  
He ate it up so quickly;  
  For each scrap he licked the ground.

My husband had gone with me
  And we said, "come home with us."
A pup so sweet and needy
  There was nothing to discuss.

At first stayed within our garage
  But later grew more bold;
Was hit and injured by a car
  When he was one year old.

We couldn't find him all that night.
  Had he gone off to die?
The rule about nine lives for cats
  To dogs might not apply.

Next day I saw him in the yard
  All stretched out on his side;
Stiff and sore and battered
  But our Buster had not died.

One night he was out roaming;
  Someone hit him very hard.
His right front leg was broken
  But he hobbled to our yard.

We gave him aspirin for the pain
  Braced his leg against a stick.
Called vets to find a friendly one
  Who would see our dog real quick.

He made a good recovery
  But his roving days were through.
We kept him on a lengthy chain;
  Took him out for long walks too.

Whenever I picked up his leash
  He was always set to go.

When we had gone a mile of two,
  He'd start to walk more slow.

Our little grandson, Jacob,
  Soon was toddling round the place.
Buster was so patient with him
  And he'd lick his hands and face.

Jacob kept on growing bigger;
  Thought of different ways to play.
With his gun kept "banging" Buster
  Till the noise drove him away.

The years were passing quickly;
  Buster's muzzle now was gray
His coat rich brown with streaks of gold
  As we walked out on Monday.

On Tuesday he seemed listless
  So I walked my route alone.
All day he was not eating;
  Didn't cough or wheeze or moan.

Sometimes he laid upon his pad
  And sometimes on the ground.
He looked at us with loving eyes
  But didn't make a sound.

This morning he was cold and stiff;
  No message we'd exchange.
Again I walked without him
  And it seemed so very strange.

I'm left with sorrow in my life;
  The portion at an end.
But I will long remember.
  This dog, my special friend.

# A DAY FOR THANKSGIVING

Another leaf in the book of life;
  Another year nearly done;
A special day for our family
  To talk, to eat, to have fun.

A day for special thanksgiving;
  For pausing to savor our wealth.
The gifts we have been given;
  Our family, possessions and health.

A day to be truly humble
  For blessings which have come our way;
For the strength and support of a Savior
  Who walks by our side day by day.

A day for revealing our feelings;
  For voicing just how much we care,
As we come to this Thanksgiving dinner
  Which all have helped to prepare.

A day for sharing together;
  Expressing thoughts from our heart.
As long as we're one in spirit,
  We truly are never apart.

A day to depart in the twilight;
  Stuffed with food and feeling content;
At peace with ourselves and each other;
  A day that's been very well spent!

# CHRISTMAS STOCKINGS

Eleven red socks upon a brick wall.
  Our family's story; they tell it all.
When originally made, there were only three;
  Names written in glitter for all to see.


Marge, Bart and Vicki, our little tot;
  She was so happy whatever she got.
Candy, an orange, and a little surprise
  Brought such a glitter to her brown eyes.


By the time she was four, she had a new brother.
  To our Christmas socks we added another.
Orders to Thailand Dad had to obey;
  But we hung our socks in the usual way.


His sock near the others; hung in a row
  Near a big wreath with a red ribbon bow.
A baby boy added, our family complete.
  Five socks on the mantle really looked neat.


In just over a year, our daughter died.
  When we hung up the stockings, we laid hers aside.
Four stockings were hung in numerous place;
  As we changed locations, and greeted new faces.

A permanent home where we now reside
  Gave us a sense of community pride.
Outdoor decorations could be viewed by all;
  But inside we saw four socks on the wall.

John and David grew up but the socks were tradition;
  No longer as bright or in tip-top condition.
When they trekked home for Christmas, they wanted to see
  Four socks on the wall hanging near a spruce tree.

As wives joined our family we welcomed them in
  And Mom was busy making stockings again.
A grandson was followed by twin sisters too.
  Then two more grandaughters, our family was through.

Five more stockings now hang on the wall.
  Jacob, Lindsey and Vicki are growing so tall.
Davida and Jemma live so far away
  But we all get together each Christmas day.

The stockings are special, a tradition so dear;
  Soon stored away till we hang them next year.
Eleven red socks upon a brick wall.
  Our family's story; they tell it all.

# MY HOMESTEAD

A ranch-style house on an overgrown lot
  With scarcely a path to the door.
The first time we turned in the driveway;
  No clue of what lay in store.

A creek ran the length of the side yard
  And trees grew all over the place.
Flowers and hostas were planted
  In every conceivable place.

I saw past the vines and the brambles;
  The thorns on the black locust tree.
With lots of hard work through each season
  It could be a dream home for me.

For thirty-eight years we kept at it;
  Investing ourselves on this land.
Now it's time to give up our homestead;
  The hourglass has run out of sand.

The yard is filled with new plantings
  I've added through all of the years.
When I think of all we've accomplished,
  It's hard to hold back the tears.

For Christmas, lights, stars and a stable
  With angels nailed to the trees.

In spring, Easter eggs and a bunny;
  In summer, flags swayed in the breeze.

With a lawn swing under the arbor;
  Eating clusters of grapes in the fall.
A wiener roast by a bonfire;
  I fondly remember it all.

Our kids going sledding or skating;
  Riding bikes on trails near the lake.
Watching meteorites crossing the night sky;
  At midnight we were still awake.

Too soon the kids were departing;
  But the cycle started anew.
When they brought their kids to grandpa's
  They were thrilled with so much to do.

Pumping water from a well in the back yard;
  Picking berries and peaches to eat;
Gathering fireflies at twilight;
  Feeling dewdrops on their bare feet.

That stage of my life is now over;
  To the passage of time I must bow.
Senior days bring more limitations;
  Major changes are facing me now.

# THE CLASS OF '53

Fifty-five years since we left CHS,
  with no clue what lay ahead.
Earthly explorations seemed over;
  but man conquered space instead.

Missions to get men in orbit,
  and then voyages off to the moon;
Followed by an inhabited station;
  will passenger flights be here soon?

We have lived through changes in culture.
  Seen Hippies with long hair and beads,
Rejecting our social conventions;
  living simply with very few needs.

Smoking hashish and marijuana,
  sprawled in a haze on the floor.
Attempting to alter our country,
  proclaiming, "Make Love, Not War."

We witnessed the Civil Rights movement,
  in our living rooms on TV screens;
The sit-ins, the marches, the riots,
  the violence pervading the scenes.

We watched the school integration;
  saw attitudes change through the years.
Obama campaigned to be president;
  Illinois supported with cheers.

Equal Rights for women, an issue,
  with demands for more jobs, better pay.
In the 50's housewives were common,
  but careers are the norm for today.

Women are doctors and lawyers;
  in business they are gaining control.
There are some women in Congress,
  and the presidency is Sarah's goal.

Our class graduated in peace time;
  in a few years we were bogged down in war.
Young men were drafted for service,
  most had a year's Vietnam tour.

Since then the draft has been ended;
  National Guard called up more and more
To fight against terrorist aggression,
  in the Afghan and Iraqi war.

When we were students in high school,
  the typewriter was status quo.
We had no concept of a future,
  with contacts wherever we go.

Technology gave us word processors,
  computers at first functioned slow.
Now with cell phones, faxes and email,
  continually we're in the know.

There have been many medical advances.
  We remember when penicillin was new.
Complicated surgeries are common;
  it's amazing what doctors can do.

There are so many organs to transplant;
  a kidney, a heart or a lung.
Things we couldn't even imagine,
  back in the days we were young.

As the world around us kept changing,
  we have made changes and grew.
We married and raised our families.
  Now our days of employment are through.

When we walked out the doors with diplomas,
  the world to us seemed fresh and new.
Fifty-five years have changed us,
  and the world has kept changing too.

# DOWNSIZING

Downsizing is a fancy term
  For getting rid of stuff.
Because we're getting older
  Bare essentials are enough.

No need for keeping souvenirs,
  Mementos from the past;
Stamps, coins or shell collections,
  Passing interests did not last.

Cupboards filled with china
  Just used on Christmas Day.
Best-selling books of fiction;
  Read once, then shelved away.

Tools for household projects
  And a garden that's no more.
Items one might use some day
  There's just no room to store.

The toys boxed in the attic
  That the children left behind.
The crafts and decorations,
  Homemade, one of a kind.

The options are quite limited
  Because the space is small;
But it's so liberating
  To throw away it all.

Forget about the time that's gone;
  Make plans to look ahead.
Don't dwell upon what used to be;
  Be positive instead.

We often get the message,
  To downsize is daring, bold;
But the ones who tout this action
  Are the young and not the old.

# MY FRIEND

Shirley was just a casual acquaintance
  That I saw at church or the store;
But through life's circumstances
  To me, she became so much more.

I was in treatment for cancer;
  I was vulnerable, frightened and weak.
Shirley drove me to medical appointments
  And encouraged me when life seemed bleak.

We shared our backgrounds and histories;
  How we both had been teenage brides;
How motherhood took full commitment;
  Babes in arms and tots by our sides.

We shared about casserole dinners
  And pay checks that were always too small.
Yet those times now seemed so special
  When we were recalling it call.

We had so much in common;
  Two women who just seemed to click.
We went from polite conversations
  To sharing emotions so quick.

We had fun shopping for bargains;
  Keeping track of what was on sale;
Saving coupons we clipped from the papers
  And others that came in the mail.

We lunched on pizza or tacos;
  Ate slowly, with so much to share.
Regardless of life's circumstances.
  For me, Shirley always was there.

Shirley set a powerful example
  Of all that a Christian should be
I'll keep her alive in my memories;
  A friend, very special to me.

# OUR LIFE TOGETHER

Fifty years is really a short time
  For God and His eternal plan;
But fifty years being married
  Is lengthy for a woman and man.

And yet the time goes so quickly;
  The days and the years moving on.
If we pause for a time of reflection,
  We ask, "Where has our life gone?"

The children were long ago grown;
  The nest has been empty for years;
Retirement has been an adjustment;
  Thoughts of the future cause fears.

Objectively, our health is waning;
  Each year we grow frailer, more weak.
If we dwell on our limitations,
  The future can only seem bleak.

Our options are fewer and fewer.
  "Shall we downsize or stay where we're at?"
We try to make careful decisions,
  "Is it best to do this or do that?"

We can only do so much planning;
  Only God knows for us what's ahead.
We must give Him our fears and our worries
  And follow His bidding instead.

The remaining years may be trying;
  And death may soon take one away;
But whatever time we are given
  Is meant for wise use day by day.

Pleasure in changing of seasons;
  Of grandkids who love us so much;
Of foods allowed on our diet;
  And old friends who still keep in touch.

With hearts that are grateful for blessings;
  Having money to pay monthly bills;
Worship in public and private;
  Tranquility instead of thrills.

Fifty years we have been together;
  With tough times but also much fun.
The time that is left is a bonus;
  For us it has been a good run.

# Life

# OUR PURPOSE

What is the purpose for living?
  Why are we placed on this earth?
Questions which all men have pondered,
  As they seek life's meaning and worth.

If we're honest, we know we are feeble;
  Our allotment of time will be small.
After death we will soon be forgotten;
  Does our life have no purpose at all?

Some choose to avoid such deep musings;
  Stay active so they won't dwell
On questions for which they've no answers.
  They pretend that their life is just swell!

When we learn about Jesus, there's answers;
  He died on the cross for our sin;
Has forgiveness for each individual
  When we open our hearts; let Him in.

In His love He will freely redeem us;
  Save our souls for time without end.
Day by day give us strength and assurance;
  He's a constant on which to depend.

He provides for today and tomorrow;
  For each circumstance or each need.
When we know Jesus Christ as our Savior,
  All of life has meaning indeed!

# ONE IN A MILLION

One in a million that's born every day.
  I seem unimportant when listed that way.

One of so many; lost in the crowd.
  I've done nothing special to make others proud.

Faceless and nameless; an anonymous being.
  I've no fame or beauty that others are seeing.

But one in a million in the image of God.
  He made us each different; not "peas in a pod."

To God we are special; not assembly line made.
  Individuals of worth whether jolly or staid.

To know that God loves me makes everything fine.
  Truly one in a million, that promise is mine.

We each one have value; unique in God's sight.
  He is always beside us regardless our plight.

Each one in a million from God hears a call.
  He invites us to seek Him; has love for us all.

Each one in a million has freedom to choose;
  To accept or reject Christ; to share the Good News.

I'm one in a million born on the same day;
  But I'm special to God, so all is okay.

# LIFE WITH MY MOTHER

Each mother and child is different
  But all are somewhat the same
Mothers take care of their children;
  Responding when they call her name.

We all recall times without mother
  On a joyous or on a sad day.
Regardless what the occasion,
  Mother always knew what to say.

I have memories of mother
  From the time I wasn't quite three.
Because she was so largely pregnant,
  I sat on the end of her knee.

After working all day, she made supper;
  I'm sure she was ready to rest.
While we waited for Dad, we would cuddle;
  The time of the day I liked best.

We went to stay at my Grandma's
  When my baby sister was born.
Everyone else was excited
  But I was feeling forlorn.

Soon we returned to our own home.
  Now I had a new role, "Big Sis."
Mom always made bedtime quite special;
  A prayer, a hug and a kiss.

I got many books for each Christmas
  And I desperately wanted to read.
At five I started the first grade;
  A time upon which Mom agreed.

Mom went with me the first day;
  Stood near by my little seat.
When I realized she had departed,
  My heart seemed to drop to my feet.

Such emptiness, loneliness, sorrow,
  Independence for me had begun.
I shared all the details with Mother
  When  each day of schoolwork was done.

As I came back home in the evening
  There was often warm bread or a pie.
A snack, chore time and then supper;
  The seasons and years soon passed by.

Mom was warm, pleasant, outgoing,
  And she couldn't see why I was shy.
She was certain I could be like her
  If I was just willing to try.

I'm sure she was disappointed;
  My social skills were so few.
But at home just with the family
  There were so many fun things to do.

Baking cookies, my FHA project,
  Was one the whole family enjoyed.
Chocolate chip was voted the favorite;
  In the kitchen I was often employed.

Mom always believed I was honest;
  On my common sense could rely.
Whatever the task she assigned me,
  I was eager to give it a try.

Mom gave me my morals and values;
  A conscience to steer me along.

Her voice would subconsciously reach me
  When I faltered or did something wrong.

As the oldest of seven siblings,
  I was first at each thing, led the way.
As I graduated from high school,
  Mom was so proud on that day.

I worked in a bank for a short time,
  Lived at home and purchased a car.
I married, began an adventure;
  Moved to Texas which seemed very far.

As an Air Force dependent I traveled
  To wherever my husband was based.
Mom and I corresponded
  And the good times and bad times we faced.

When I gave birth to my children,
  My purpose in life was revealed.
Mom loved her role as a Grandma;
  Our bond was more firmly sealed.

When my daughter was taken from us,
  We questioned why she should die.
Mom and I went to our Bibles;
  In God's word we found a reply.

"My ways are not yours" was the answer
  Which helped me to trust and believe.
Mom read to be patient and wait on the Lord
  New strength from the Lord she'd receive.

With time Mom's limbs have now weakened
  But the love which we share is the same.
She is honored by all of her family,
  "Dearest Mother" is her special name.

# A SPECIAL CHRISTMAS

Which was my most special Christmas?
  I pause and take time to reflect.
With memories from so many seasons,
  Which is the one to select?

The Christmas which I first remember
  Was when I was almost age three.
My earnest request to Santa Claus was,
  "Please bring many books just for me."

I loved preparations for Christmas;
  Being cast in a pageant or play.
Acting the role of another
  And telling a story that way.

I learned there is much joy in giving
  A gift, no matter how small.
With eight in immediate family,
  It was hard to buy gifts for them all.

We always had candy and oranges;
  Made popcorn most every night.
As we sat near the glow of our wood-burning stove,
  We were warm and our world was all right.

We had our traditions and customs;
  Ways of making the season our own.
I carried this family lore with me
  Through the years when I was grown.

There was great joy in repeating
  These customs all over this land;
In giving my children a stable domain;
  Often moving at Air Force command.

I remember the snowfall in England;
  So rare we could scarcely believe.
It covered all of the landscape;
  A miracle on Christmas Eve.

I remember a year when we traveled
  To see all the wonders of Spain.
We watched a parade on Epiphany;
  Relived Christmas magic again.

But the Christmas which is the most vivid
  Was the year my daughter had died.
I dreaded the joy of the season;
  But for all my family, I tried.

I just went through all the motions;
   Bought the present, put up the tree.
Christmas Eve I heard "The Messiah"
   And the music and words set me free.

I came to a time of acceptance;
   I had to go on with God's aid.
I felt God lift the pain from my heart;
   Give me peace to move on unafraid.

Her memory will always be with me.
   I remember the ten years we shared.
But because she believed in the Savior,
   For death she was fully prepared.

I'm compelled at the holiday season
   To proclaim God's love for mankind;
To pray that the lost or the troubled
   God's love and forgiveness will find.

Christmas is my affirmation
   That the things I believe are so true.
And although I gave up my daughter
   God gave up His Son for us too.

# THE PURPOSE OF LIFE

There is a natural order to life;
  Progression each step of the way.
Death is the inevitable ending;
  Approaching more closely each day.

Life begins for an infant
  And onward through childhood he grows.
Then teen-agers turn into adults
  And faster and faster life goes.

As young adults become parents,
  The cycle of life starts anew.
Each generation moves onward
  Until their lifetime is through.

Grandparents thrill to have grandkids
  To see their line carried on;
To know family life will continue
  When this generation is gone.

Births, graduations, and weddings
  Are events that happen each year.
They suddenly have special meaning
  When involving a loved one so dear.

We need to take time for reflection;
  To study the lifespan of man,
To look for the ultimate answer;
  Have hope through God's life-changing plan.

By putting our faith in the Savior,
  There's new life beyond earthly time.
Reunions with loved ones in Heaven;
  No worries, no sorrow, no crime.

Eternity filled with rejoicing!
  To God we will lift up our praise!
The light will always surround us;
  Celebration throughout endless days!

This hope gives life a purpose;
  Assurance we can persevere.
By trusting in Jesus the Savior
  We can live without worry or fear.

# TRUE THANKSGIVING

True thankfulness is more than emotion;
  It comes from the depth of the heart.
To catalog some of my blessings,
  I wonder where I should start.

I'm thankful for all of creation;
  The wonders of nature God made.
When I work in the heat of the summer,
  I'm thankful for tall trees with shade.

I'm thankful for sunrise and sunset;
  Beginning and end of each day.
Lengths may vary by seasons
  But progress in an orderly way.

I'm thankful for beautiful rainbows;
  The colors arched over the sky.
Reminder of all God has promised;
  A covenant we can live by.

I'm so thankful that God loves me;
  And He knew me before I was born.
We each are made in His likeness.
  We are worthy; not objects to scorn.

I'm thankful for my salvation;
  Adversity caused me to trust.
I'm seeking God's will for me daily
  Accepting hard times when I must.

I'm thankful that God's always with me;
  Won't load me with too much to bear.
I feel his comforting presence
  When I'm in the depths of despair.

I'm thankful for all of my family;
  My husband, grandchildren, sons.
Two "daughters" welcomed through marriage;
  God selected for us the right ones.

I'm thankful for my church family;
  Relationships strengthened through years.
An unspoken bond between us
  In happiness, sorrow or tears.

I'm thankful God has sustained me;
  Given training and helped me to grow.
Gave me courage to reach out to people
  And allow my true feelings to show.

I'm thankful for all of my travels;
   Spending time in assortment of places.
In Africa, Europe and Asia
   I've learned of the cultures and races.

I'm thankful for those who defend us,
   The soldiers protecting our land;
Fighting tyrants, dictators, insurgents,
   Whatever the need may demand.

I'm thankful that we have a Bible
   Assuring us God is in charge.
We see "as through a glass darkly"
   Because the landscape's too large.

But God sees and knows the whole picture;
   His ways and ours not the same.
I'm so thankful to put my trust in Him;
   In Heaven He has staked my claim.

I'm thankful for this special season
   To pause, to give thanks and reflect
How often my prayers have been answered;
   More blessings than I could expect.

# THE WORTH OF A FRIEND

The worth of a friend is priceless;
  A friend who converses and shares.
Whether in joy or in sorrow,
  A friend empathizes and cares.

A real friend is never too busy
  To respond to our problems or woe.
True friendship transcends time and distance;
  Is a comfort wherever we go.

A true friend accepts us and loves us;
  Through encouragement brings out our best;
Gives us the faith and the courage
  To face any problem or test.

A true friend's devotion is constant;
  Is the same in a crowd or alone.
One should count it a blessing
  To have such a friend as his own.

The Bible gives an example,
  Jonathon, rich son of a king
And David, musician and shepherd,
  Shared friendship, a most precious thing.

A greater example is Jesus;
  No better friend one can find.
He died to give mankind redemption;
  Such friendship is one of a kind.

Earthly friendships are needed;
  We all desire friends of our own.
When lonely, we still are not friendless;
  With Jesus we are never alone.

# A FIFTY YEAR JOURNEY

I have been a believer
  And followed the Lord fifty years.
My faith in God has triumphed
  Through adversities, losses and fears.

I gave my life to the Savior
  To follow His leading, obey.
Finding my place of service
  Committed the whole course to stay.

I wanted the best for my children
  So they were in church every week;
Memorizing verses of scripture,
  Seeking answers for which we all seek.

I saw them all come to the Savior;
  One go to her heavenly home.
Two sons now raising five children;
  Each claiming Christ's gift as their own.

Hindsight is better than foresight;
  Looking back I've been blessed many ways.
As I come to the end of my sojourn,
  In heaven I'll dwell endless days.

# OUR TRUE WORTH

In the overall picture of life on this earth
  We are insignificant, small.
Our role is minute, just a second in time.
  A blip  on the screen, that is all.

We strive for personal greatness
  But there is no lasting fame.
In just a few generations
  No one will remember our name.

This life is only a preview
  Of eternal life that's to be.
Jesus provides that assurance.
  He forgives us; from sin sets us free.

We tend to think we have personal worth;
  Our egos are out of control.
We need to accept how puny we are;
  Without Christ, we cannot be whole.

Our possessions have no lasting value
  Will dwindle to ashes or dust.
The auto that's so bright and shiny
  Will some day be covered with rust.

The tombstone containing our history
  Is etched with details of our being;
But the printing will dim through the ages
  And our life facts no one will be seeing.

When we face the fact of how short our time,
  It gives us a different objective.
It gives us cause to question our goals
  When viewed from a different perspective.

# ONE CHANCE

We only get one chance in life.
  One chance to do it right,
To nurture our small children;
  Tuck them in their beds each night.


One chance for family outings;
  For vacations to recall.
For holiday traditions
  Observed by one and all.


One chance for moral training;
  For teaching right from wrong.
For directing to good choices
  As we steer young folks along.


One chance for preparations
  For a child to live alone
As they gain their independence
  When they are fully grown.


One chance to lead along the way
  To set a good example
Through all of life's discouragement;
  With faith that's deep and ample.

# THE SEEDS OF LIFE

Children's lives are anchored
  By the seeds their Mothers plant;
Seeds which also may be planted
  By a Grandma or an Aunt.

Seeds of truth and honesty;
  Of knowing what is right;
Of doing what is proper
  When Mom is not in sight.

Seeds for the joy of learning;
  For the knowledge found in books;
Resources on the internet
  Research for which one looks.

Seeds of determination
  To see a project through.
One's word is his commitment;
  What's promised one must do.

Seeds of deep compassion,
  Caring and concern.
With Mother as a model
  These habits children learn.

Seeds of thrifty habits;
  Learning how to save and spend.
Making wise investments;
  Not obsessed by every trend.

Seeds for travel and adventure
  To experience new things.
To step outside "one's comfort zone"
  To which one often clings

Seeds of pride in country
  And the stars and stripes which wave.
Pride in all our soldiers;
  Patriotic, loyal and brave.

Seeds of good behavior
  Begun when very small;
"Excuse me, please, and thank you;"
  The polite child knows them all.

Seeds of faith in Jesus
  As a Savior and a friend.
Faith that is sustaining
  From life's start until its end.

Seeds of love and tenderness
  Through years of life will grow.
With time they will grow stronger;
  Love's reflection they will show.

The good seeds mothers choose to plant
  Will lodge in children's hearts.
The very day a child is born
  Is when the gardening starts.

Seeds may be slow in growing
  And Mothers may despair.
But seedlings will be sprouting
  Due to nurture and good care.

The plants that will develop
  In the future, fruit will bear.
Through succeeding generations
  Mother's truths her children share.

# GO FOR IT !

We need a dream, a vision,
  What God would have us do.
It's worth a lengthy time of toil
  When the goal is in our view.

Hardships and disappointments
  May hinder or delay;
But treasures worth possessing
  Are worth the price we pay.

Anything worth having
  Is worth the time required;
Believing in a lofty goal
  To which we have aspired.

Focus on what's meaningful;
  The cherished hope pursue.
There is no guarantee in life
  But God will see us through.

Failure is never final;
  The challenge we can meet.
By ever pressing onward,
  We can overcome defeat.

# Faith

# IN GOD'S HOUSE

I've traveled all across this land
  And lived in foreign places;
Adjusting to a whole new scene;
  New homes, new schools, new faces.

And often near our Air Force Base
  We found a welcome sight;
A friendly Southern Baptist Church;
  It filled us with delight.

At first the folks were strangers
  And some customs might seem odd.
But there was a common interest,
  We had fellowship with God.

As we worshiped in the Spirit,
We were very much aware
That we were all God's children
  And His blessings we could share.

We made friends in all those places
  That we shall see no more;
Until we are all together
  When we enter Heaven's door.

I'm thankful for the knowledge
  I can serve God anywhere.
Wherever Christians worship,
  A loving God is there.

I'm thankful for my Christian friends.
  This church which nurtures me.
The bond of love which binds us
  Throughout eternity.

# THE CHURCH OF GOD

The church is never the building;
  It's the people who gather within;
People who choose to serve Jesus
  Who loves them and saves them from sin.

The church assembles to worship
  God, the creator of all,
Designer of Eden, perfection,
  Before man was tempted to fall.

The church assembles to study
  The Testaments, both old and new.
In the Old one Messiah is foretold
  With prophecies what He would do.

The New one leads us to Jesus;
  A deity, both God and man,
A Savior who died to redeem us,
  Fulfillment of God's chosen plan.

The church reaches out to all people;
  Welcomes those who are burdened, alone.
No one is perfect but Jesus;
  If we ask, He will make us His own.

The people of God have a mission
  To share the Savior they've found.
The world is filled with the needy;
  There are unaware folks all around.

God's people know He is unchanging.
  His message through time stays the same.
There is only one route to Heaven;
  Seeking Jesus and calling His name.

# SINGING TO HONOR GOD

I come to Sunday worship
  And I raise my voice in song.
I have no formal training
  But I've known these hymns so long.

These hymns bring back the memories
  Of places where I've been;
The Christians that I worshiped with
  And hope to meet again.

I learned hymns as a little child
  With a rural congregation.
Their daily chores and farm work
  Made church seem like vacation.

I sang hymns with my family;
  Children nestled in my lap
And when the sermon started
  They often took a nap.

I sang hymns with my special friend;
  Our voices seemed to blend.
We had no indication
  How soon her life would end.

Hymns may have words of comfort;
  To meet a special need
To overcome discouragement
  And help me to succeed.

I sing hymns when I'm driving;
  I may modify the song;
Or do many repetitions
  As I'm traveling along.

Hymns are in my background;
  Part of all the things I know.
They linger in my conscience;
  Travel with me where I go.

I raise my voice with gusto
  And I know my singing's loud.
It reminds me of my Mother
  She could be heard in a crowd.

Until her death she sang old hymns
  Her voice still clear and strong.
Perhaps she joins my melodies
  With a Heavenly sing-along.

# MOTHER TAUGHT ME HOW TO PRAY

My mother taught me how to pray;
  Tucked me in bed at close of day.
This prayer gave peace, assurance too
  Of all the things that God could do.
Sometimes I'd add a personal plea
  Concerning things that were bothering me.

As I grew older, I hungered for more.
  I lost the contentment that I'd had before.
I was a sinner; I knew it was true
  Pride kept me from confessing as I needed to do.
In private I'd pray for forgiveness of sin
  And in a few nights I would do it again.

I grew up and married, had children too.
  For them I pledged all the best things I'd do.
I took them to church when they were still small;
  Made a public profession, committed my all.
What a season of joy, I thanked God in  prayer.
  When I was baptized, I was walking on air.

I've had study sessions of the right way to pray;
  But God knows my heart, not just what I say.
God wants to hear from us, all through the day.

He wants us to praise Him, heed His will and obey.
He wants us to share the concerns of our heart;
  To seek His direction when a project we start.

God is there for us from the start to the end.
  However life's going, on Him we depend.
Each prayer will be answered, in the way God sees fit.
  It may require patience, as we wait for a bit.
We sometimes may question, our vision is small;
  But God is all-Knowing, and He sees it all.

Look beyond our church family and our physical needs.
  Pray for direction wherever God leads.
Pray for our city, our state, and our nation.
  Pray for all people they are God's creation.
Prayer spurs us to action, we must stay on the track.
  Commit to God's service and never look back.

God gives us talents to use for His glory.
  We can have a small part in a marvelous story;
Providing the means to help people know
  That Jesus died for them and He loves them so.
Improvements in methods we proudly may claim
  But the need to keep praying is always the same.

# GOD'S CALL

Across the endless years of time,
  God has called out to man
To fellowship, commune with Him;
  From Adam, "twas His plan."

God calls each for salvation
  With erasure of our sin.
He gives us choice and freedom
  As He seeks to draw us in.

God calls each one to service
  That the church can do its task.
He gives us skills and talents
  To accomplish what he'll ask.

God calls each one to Heaven;
  A home planned and prepared.
As death ends earthly sojourn,
  His mansion to be shared.

God calls each one directly;
  Seeks an answer to His plea.
When we stall or make excuses,
  He asks, "Won't you come to me?"

God's call is liberating;
  It absolves and sets us free.
We are saved for life's brief moment
  And throughout eternity.

# TRUST AND ACCEPT

When I was still a teen-age girl,
  I'd ponder "what's ahead?"
Mom said, "it's better not to know;
  Just trust in God instead."

"Enjoy the repetitious tasks;
  The day-to-day routine;
For change can come so suddenly;
  Wreak havoc on the scene."

"Not knowing what awaits us
  Helps us not to live in dread;
Surrounded by our family's love
  We'll face what lies ahead."

Mom had no education
  But she was truly wise.
An unexpected tragedy
  Is always great surprise.

When death strikes a family,
  It shatters, tears apart.
The pain we feel is so intense;
  It almost breaks our heart.

Our first reaction, disbelief;
  Denial, "NO! NO! NO!"
Then overcome with waves of grief.
  We must accept it though.

There's pleasure in the memories
When a dear one's life is past
And we know that time is fleeting
  Each life moves on so fast.

In pain we are prone to cry out "why?"
  "Why did God let this be?"
But in the midst of darkness
  A small light we may see.

A little light to give us hope;
  A reminder God is near.
If we share our inmost thoughts with Him,
  He's listening and will hear.

As long as we dwell on this earth
  There's much that we won't know;
But God sustains us through our pain
  And helps our faith to grow.

We cannot know tomorrow;
  We can't see beyond today;
But whatever lies before us
  God is with us all the way.

We see darkly through a glass;
  The future is not clear;
But we can place our trust in God
  He's always with us here.

God's ways are not our ways;
  They are higher than our reach
But we are God's children
  And He has love for each.

# WHEN LIFE DOESN'T MAKE SENSE

When life doesn't make sense
  To our finite mind;
When God no longer
  Seems loving and kind.

When life overwhelms us
  With sorrow and pain;
When we think we will
  Never be happy again.

When life doesn't make sense,
  Logic does not apply.
When we can't understand,
  Then our question is "why?"

Jesus also asked why
  When to a cross nailed.
He felt so forsaken
  But God's will prevailed.

When there is no answer,
  To God we must turn.
His plan or His purpose
  We later may learn.

God gives us the strength
  To accept and endure;
To live with affliction
  When there is no cure.

God gives us assurance
  That things work for good.
If we're called for His purpose;
  Love Him as we should.

There will always be times
  When life doesn't make sense.
We must trust in the Lord,
  Not blame; take offense.

The Lord in His mercy
  Will lead and will guide.
If we love Him and praise Him,
  He'll stay by our side.

# BEING A WARRIOR

To be a warrior on the wall
  Requires some dedication;
A willingness to clear an hour
  For prayer and contemplation.

But Satan tempts in little ways;
  On Tuesday nights I'm tired.
In the tasks of daily living
  I'm bogged down, completely mired.

The thought of going off to bed
  Is often a temptation;
But my "hour of prayer" commitment
  Was for a long duration.

I gather Bible, worship aids;
  Retreat to God in prayer
With praises and petitions,
  Private thoughts I want to share.

I read verses from the Bible
  Through which I hear God speak.
As I marvel at His greatness,
  He gives answers which I seek.

I beseech God for His mighty power
   To move across this land;
To touch the hearts of sinful men
   So Revival fires are fanned.

I pledge that I'll be faithful;
   Steadfastly I will wait
 For God to make the changes
   I expect, anticipate.

God has his own timetable
   But when Christians kneel and pray
He will surely hear and answer
   Let Revival come our way.

How fast the whole hour passes;
   I regret to have it end;
To close my conversation
   With Jesus Christ, my friend.

# GOD'S PLAN

God knows our every thought.
  He knows our reasons too.
He cares about our motives;
  Not just the things we do.

He sees through our actions
  If our motives are not right.
We must be humble servants
  To be righteous in His sight.

In haughty pride and arrogance
  We brag about our deeds.
We run in all direction
  Not seeking where God leads.

We want a place of honor;
  Respect on earth from man.
What will we do to gain it?
  Will we go against God's plan?

When I become rebellious
  I deny God's plan for me;
Not seeking my Lord's guidance;
  What to do or what to be.

Denial of my Savior
  Always leads to woe and pain.
Then I ask Him for forgiveness
  And I'm right with him again.

# FREEDOM THROUGH CHRIST

Independence is not total freedom
  From morals and ethics and laws.
Before making hasty decisions
  We need to consider and pause.

Will this action benefit others?
  Is this what God wants us to be?
Are we standing for truth and for justice?
  Or are we absorbed with just "me?"

With freedom comes limited boundaries;
  Perimeters in which we should dwell.
Committing to God and His service;
  With faith that all will be well.

Freedom in Christ gives assurance
  Of peace and of life without end.
Adversities may overtake us
  But we will not break, only bend.

Freedom through Christ is forever;
  Endless life in a holy domain.
When this earth becomes non-existent,
  God's Heavenly realm will remain.

# MY GOAL

We are God's own creation;
  He knows when we're burdened or weak.
He deals with our flaws to improve us;
  When a life that is righteous, we seek.


We are unique, each one different;
  Have emotions that sometimes control.
Each family's dynamic is different;
  Each member filling a role.


I come from a poor, rural family;
  The eldest, and often in charge
Of household tasks and my siblings.
  My burdens seemed heavy and large.


I lived by the rules, did the right things;
  I held my head high, appeared proud.
I was remote, isolated;
  Even when part of a crowd.


I chose not to bow before Jesus;
  God touched me and made me aware
My pride was a sin needing humbled.
  When I faced it forgiveness was there.

Pride still is my weakness;
  God helps me to grow day by day.
I find little ways I can serve Him.
  What He commands, I obey.

I utilize what I've been given;
  Baking cookies for other to share;
Planning outings for older church members;
  Sensing needs and showing I care.

Listening in times of bereavement;
  Helping by just being there;
Encouraging friends to be faithful
  And lifting them up through my prayer.

I seek God's will in my routine;
  Many years on Him I've relied.
I have no cause to be prideful;
  My goal is Christ glorified.

# HOW TO DO IT BETTER?

"How to do it better"
  Is what we want to know.
We strive for self-improvement
  No matter where we go.

Perhaps we want to learn a skill
  To aid in our career;
Or take up public speaking
  To overcome our fear.

"How to do it better!"
  There's advice in many books
On how to choose our wardrobes
  Or glamorize our looks.

"How to do it better"
  Can be of great concern;
But if we follow Jesus
  The best way we can learn.

So many things in this world
  Are just a passing fad.
We need to analyze our goals.
  Are they for good or bad?

Jesus has the master pattern
  On which our life to build;
If we seek His guidance,
  Our spirits will be filled.

# GOD'S WILL FOR US?

A question Christians often ask:
  What is God's will for me?
What should I be doing?
  Where would you have me be?

We watch for special feelings.
  A vision or a sign.
Each wants a deep encounter
  That is uniquely mine.

We want some fun, excitement
  When daily life's a bore.
It may be what God's planned for us
  But we want something more.

Our present job may be God's will;
  The thing He'd have us do.
While we want to change direction,
  Be a part of something new.

If we have no firm directive,
  We should just stay on our route.
To firmly stay the course with God
  Is what life's all about.

# WITH GOD AS YOUR PARTNER

You are called! You have gifts!
  What would God have you do?
Can you preach or teach or witness?
  What is God's plan for you?


You have the greatest partner
  To lead you every day.
"You are a laborer with God;"
  He's with you all the way.


Listen to your partner!
  Heed the urgings from your heart.
He will surely direct you;
  But you have to do your part.


God has a plan for people;
  A purpose for mankind;
He wants to reach out to the lost
  To search, to seek, to find.


God chose to have you share His work
  So you can share the joy
Each time a soul is won for Him
  Man, woman, girl, or boy.

So use the gifts God gave you;
   Know His purpose and His plan.
With God, an unseen partner,
   Accomplish all you can.

You have a special calling;
   A task that's just for you.
Search out the special mission
   Which God would have you do.

Glorify your Savior
   By your lifestyle every day!
Let your partner guide you
   When you work and when you play.

Rejoice that you are special,
   Unique, one of a kind;
With God your unseen partner
   Contentment you will find.

# CONTENTMENT

In whatsoever state I'm in,
  Therein I'll be content.
I'll do the best I can each day
  So my time is well spent.

Not wasting time bemoaning
  The things that might have been;
Not searching for life's answers
  The "why," the "how," the "when."

Not letting greed and envy
  Cause me always to want more;
Just accepting all life's blessings
  Without trying to keep score.

With a spirit of contentment
  I'll find joy in every day.
I'll see in God's creation
  Treasures which He gave away.

Working at the job I'm given
  Until every task is through;
Being thankful for my fitness
  And the work that I can do.

Contentment gives me inner peace
  Each day brings simple pleasure;
By looking for the good in life
  I find it in full measure.

# MY PRAYER

I'm very poor at public prayer;
  My thoughts become a jumble.
My sentences are incomplete;
  I hesitate and mumble.

I'm glad God knows my every thought;
  The prayers I do not voice.
I'm glad He gave me talents
  According to His choice.

I seem to have abilities
  For sharing thoughts in rhymes.
The words which I put into verse
  Express my thoughts and times.

I consolidate the sermons
  Into capsules to recall.
I believe life has a purpose
  And I thank God for it all.

I praise God for nature
  And the glories I behold.
In prayer I am bashful;
  But in writing I am bold.

I thank God for this talent
  It's my finest way to share;
To glorify my Christ in poems
  And fashion them as prayer.

# A SPECIAL BLESSING

Give me a special blessing
  Was my recent plea to God.
My desires were not specific;
  Looking back, that was quite odd.

I hoped God would send a buyer
  For a house that's hard to sell.
But, of course, there's other blessings
  God could give to me as well.

One day when I was mowing
  And the grass had grown quite high,
I spotted mushrooms in the weeds,
  Morels to pick and fry.

More than 30 mushrooms
  Where they'd never grown before,
Was that my special blessing
  That I'd been praying for?

I'll admit to disappointment.
  Was this all that is in store?
I was thrilled to find the mushrooms
  But I really needed more.

Who am I to question?
  God has a plan for me?
The mushrooms were delicious;
  I'm still waiting patiently.

# MY CREDO

"In whatsoever state I'm in
  Therein I'll be content."
When I claimed that special verse
  Those words I truly meant.

I used them as me credo
  Whenever problems came.
Though times are sometimes difficult
  I'm God's child just the same.

They gave me peace, assurance
  Everything would be okay.
When my son moved to Korea
  Which was half a world away.

They gave me hope and courage
  When cancer struck me down.
Saw me through the daily treatments
  Helped me not to mope or frown.

The treatment was successful
  And right now I'm cancer free.
But I have no way of knowing
  What lies ahead of me.

I fear what is uncertain
  Things which I cannot control.
But I can know contentment
  Because Jesus saved my soul.

Life is so precarious
  So daily I shall pray
That whatsoever state I'm in
  I'll be content today.

# TAKING INVENTORY

One does more reminiscing
  The older that one gets;
And life is so much better
  If one has no regrets.

Regrets for things one rashly said;
  For cruel remarks one made.
For not witnessing of the Savior,
  Because one was afraid.

Not standing for convictions
  But agreeing with the crowd.
Not wishing to be different,
  To express God's truth aloud.

The things that seemed so vital
  Lose importance in old age.
One sees life much more clearly;
  Has more wisdom at this stage.

One can't go back to change things;
  To set the record straight;
But one can change his lifestyle
  Before it is too late.

To ask God for forgiveness
  And to ask one's brother too;
To use Christ as the model
  For the things that one should do.

Not wasting time regretting
  The failures of past days;
But letting Christ live in one
  To be seen through all one's ways.

# MY WITNESS

When I recall my childhood
  There is much that I can share.
I was always shy and timid;
  Yet quick to take a dare.

I'd jump across the creek bed
  Or walk on a bridge rail;
Crawl through a rusty culvert
  Or explore a deep woods trail.

Within my family circle
  I was quick to share my view.
I was bossy when I baby-sat;
  Telling siblings what to do.

When my mom and aunts were talking,
  I would listen to them chat;
But when my Mom had other guests,
  She'd ask, "Where's Marjorie at?"

I'd be reading in the closet;
  Finding pleasure in a book;
Or sitting on the creek bank
  In a sheltered little nook.

I'd be climbing to the treetops
  When the cherries were bright red;
Or dreaming in the haymow.
  Straw bales made a cozy bed.

In school I was quite timid
  And I feared to speak aloud.
Because of my timidity,
  Some kids thought I was proud.

If mom heard me complaining,
  She would tell me what to do.

"Smile and be real friendly;
  Others will respond to you."

I married, had three children;
  Functioned in an Air Force life;
But I still felt so inadequate;
  As mother, and as wife.

Then I became a Christian;
  But a very timid one.
Life was serious business;
  Work came ahead of fun.

And then the worst thing happened.
  My child, aged ten, was killed.
As I stood beside her coffin
  My mouth with words was filled.

I told of my utter assurance;
  With Jesus she had gone to dwell.
Because she'd accepted the Savior,
  She was destined for Heaven, not Hell.

I reminded each one we have options;
  We must choose before it's too late.
Disease or an unforeseen happening
  May at any time seal our fate.

I had wanted the best for my children;
  Introduced them to God and His Son.
She had claimed Jesus Christ as her Savior;
  Now her earthly sojourn was done.

I don't want to be dull and boring;
  But I have a message to share.
For each of us death will be coming;
  Now is the time to prepare.

# FAITH CAN BE OUR TICKET

We all must come to terms with death;
  It's something we must face.
We can't make substitutions;
  No one can take our place.

Our time to die is coming;
  Each day it grows more near.
Everyone must face it
  And it's natural to fear.

We never get an email
  From those who've gone before.
When death has claimed a loved one,
  We hear from them no more.

There's no on-the-scene reporting;
  No news team on the spot.
Deceased ones are not interviewed
  To tell us of their lot.

But faith can be our ticket
  To reach the other side.
We have not seen; but we believe
  For each of us Christ died.

Death is an endless mystery;
  A curtain we pass through.
The end of time upon this earth
  Awaiting life anew.

# TRAVEL

Do you like new experiences
　Like traveling to strange places?
Do you like eating different foods
　With folks of foreign races?

Do you like new experiences?
　Is adventure in your veins?
Have you flown on jumbo airplanes
　Or rode on Amtrak trains?

I like such adventures;
　But it sure is nice to know
The Lord is always with me
　No matter where I go.

The ultimate adventure
　Is a trip that's still ahead;
When God calls me to Heaven
　And my earthly shell is dead.

# LIFE AFTER DEATH

To be absent from the body
  Is to be with Christ our Lord.
Throughout our lifetime journey,
  It's the goal we work toward.

It's the hope on which we focus
  When we suffer grief or pain.
Though death now separates us,
  We will see loved ones again.

As our bodies serve no purpose,
  We will shed them when we die.
An earthly illustration:
  From a moth to butterfly.

Our bodies as we know them
  Are nothing but a shell.
They are temporary lodgings
  Till with Jesus Christ we dwell.

# HEAVEN WILL BE FINAL

Heaven will be final;
  No travel to and fro.
A stable situation;
  We'll never pack and go.

We'll meet and greet each other;
  Know those we've never met.
Exchanging warm affection;
  Such pleasure we will get.

We'll have no pain or trouble;
  No time that's filled with stress.
Just praising and rejoicing
  At a permanent address.

Heaven will be special;
  Beyond comprehension.
A city built of precious jewels;
  Of limitless dimension.

Heaven is so wondrous;
  Yet open to us all.
We receive our reservation
  When on our Lord we call.

We have a home in Heaven;
  Jesus said it, so it's true.
A mansion for our dwelling place
  When life on earth is through.

## **Marge Alumbaugh**

### *(1936 - 2016)*

Marge lived an unusual life – from her early years in a log cabin and attending a one-room country school to world travels. She lived in many different places, visiting all of the lower forty-eight states, as well as most European nations, Israel, South Korea, and South Africa. Her life spanned the Great Depression to the War in Afghanistan, as a a military wife, sister, and mother, and the oldest of seven siblings.

She drew inspiration from everyday life and the beauty of nature, but her poetry also captured her patriotism and her love for God, providing a glimpse of the inner strength that sustained her, which was her faith.

Photo Credit: Olan Mills

# Afterward

As reflected in her poetry, Marge enjoyed the experiences her travels provided and looked forward to each new season.

Her varied interests included gardening - working in her many gardens; sewing - making dresses, costumes, and curtains; baking - famous for her butter cookies she decorated for special occasions, or "just because;" and keeping up with the "currents" - latest fashion trends, books on the best-seller lists, and world events.

Marge valued music, art, culture and learning, and her home conveyed her personality with items from the places she had lived or traveled, family keepsakes to elicit the stories vital to keeping tradition alive, and bits and pieces of whatever flair her current "project" required in the way of paint, seedlings, fabric scraps, or bricks and boards.

Her home was always welcoming to friends, family, strangers, and strays. She provided nourishment for the mind, body, and soul, serving quick wit, friendly competition (especially with word games and trivia), or feedback and tutoring in any subject needed... along with wisdom, compassionate ears and hands, and sound advice anchored by faith.

Proceeds from *Marge's Musings* will be donated, in accordance
with Marge's wishes, to Southern Baptist Missions
as a tribute to the faith of her child, Vicki Jo,
who supported the Lottie Moon ministry with pennies
she collected and saved for her Sunday School class.

www.ingramcontent.com/pod-product-compliance
Lightning Source LLC
Chambersburg PA
CBHW032006050726
47590CB00006B/2063